Wild
at
Heart

Aliénor le Gouvello

Translated by Catherine de Saint Phalle,
with photography by Cat Vinton

Affirm
press

Affirmpress
books that leave an impression

First published by Affirm Press in 2021
This edition published in 2022
Boon Wurrung Country
28 Thistlethwaite Street,
South Melbourne, VIC 3205
affirmpress.com.au
10 9 8 7 6 5 4 3 2 1

A catalogue record for this
book is available from the
National Library of Australia

Title: Wild At Heart / Aliénor le Gouvello, author.
ISBN: 9781922711694 (paperback)

Cover design by Emily Thiang
Typeset in 13/21 Adobe Garamond Pro by J&M Typesetting
Proudly printed in Australia by McPherson's Printing Group

MIX
Paper from
responsible sources
FSC® C001695

To my mother,
without whom this wouldn't have seen the light of day.

'But the real travellers are those who leave for
leaving's sake; their hearts are light as balloons,
they never diverge from the path of their fate and,
without knowing why, always say, "Let's go."'

Charles Baudelaire
'The Voyage', *Flowers of Evil*

Contents

The Bicentennial
National Trail

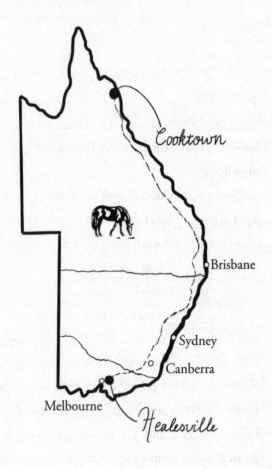

Cooktown

Brisbane

Sydney

Canberra

Melbourne

Healesville

Prologue

I travelled Australia from south to north, from Healesville to Cooktown spilling my fair share of blood along the way. Crippling pain and tropical fevers dogged my footsteps. Sometimes my joints and hands still feel as if they are being torpedoed.

Twice, staphylococci took residence in my foot and in my leg. I came just shy of contracting sepsis. During my two stays in hospital, the doctors tried to forbid me from returning to the Trail – but it didn't stop me.

My only truth was in sticking with it, for thirteen months, in all weather, through mountains and every other type of terrain. My one mission, for myself and my horses, was to find our way, to find water, food and to organise the logistics for contacting the people whose territories we were crossing. Every day, after assembling my bivouac the night before, I'd dismantle it and get myself going again: this was my routine. But my most important task was centred around my three companions. As we travelled deeper into the land, the connection between me and my horses grew exponentially. Keeping them in good physical condition, as we travelled across 5330 kilometres of land, became my strongest motivation, my underlying challenge. I did not know it at the time, but caring for them, focusing on them, is what kept me together.

1

A Long Preparation

My heart is beating much too fast. I'm hanging from the top of the round yard's guardrail. I've just been charged by my wild horse – all yawning mouth, bared teeth, bloodshot eyes and flattened ears. He would have won fights in the wild.

It's a close shave. Erica is yelling at me: *He won that round!* I must go straight back, but I'm not that keen. I baptised this eight-year-old stallion 'Guy'. He was captured in the Guy Fawkes River National Park, which is teeming with wild horses. It's odd to have named a large natural park after such a person, though. Guy Fawkes would be called a terrorist today. I learnt that he had tried to kill the Protestant king James I by stacking kegs of gunpowder under the British Houses of Parliament in London. Guy Fawkes was caught, tortured and condemned to death. At the last minute, he escaped a more grisly end by throwing himself off the scaffold and breaking his neck. The idea of using a rebel's name for this national park perhaps doesn't feel so strange after all. I do imagine my stallion Guy leaping off a scaffold …

Well, my own four-legged terrorist represents a third of my aspirations – he is, I hope, one of the three horses destined to bring my crazy dream into reality: that of crossing Australia on the Bicentennial National Trail (BNT) with wild horses.

The trek is one of the toughest in the world, and the longest in Australia. From south to north, its 5330 kilometres follow the Great Dividing Range, along the east coast, with peaks of more than 1600 metres in altitude. It crosses three states, eighteen national parks, and fifty-three ancient state forests with a unique diversity of flora and fauna.

With the help of the Guy Fawkes Heritage Horse Association, I've been trying to gain Guy's trust and tame him for two weeks. For the last two months, I've been staying at a farm, in Dorrigo – about 610 kilometres north-west of Sydney – belonging to Erica and Graeme, the founders of the association. My goal is to learn how to train wild horses – something I've never done before. Now, I gather myself and take a deep breath before returning into the round yard, even if Erica's yelling frightens me as much as the stallion. Taming a wild horse is about learning his or her language, so that you can communicate with them, speak to them – create a bond of trust. But Guy, captured at an age when he already had a taste of freedom, remains very dominant, even though he has been gelded.

Erica, observing Guy's quietness in the yards, had picked him out as perfect for training. It appears now, though, that his attitude springs more from a dominant temperament than a gentle one. When I ask too much of him, he turns and bites without warning, kicks me or charges with bared teeth. I look at Guy, motionless in a cloud of grey dust after this last charge. The oblique sunlight catches and ignites his golden buckskin coat, his baleful eyes, the drops of sweat flying from his nostrils. He's waiting for my next move. Time is flying by – and I can't venture into the bush with an intractable, unpredictable horse. My expedition is going to be taxing enough as it is. Several days later I make the decision, and give up the idea of adopting him.

I've always had a fascination for these beings who have returned to the wild. I first encountered them in the bush, in the Aboriginal communities where I worked for twelve years. It was in Docker River, a community west of Uluru, that I saw my first brumby stallion, in his shining black coat, along with his immaculate white mare. I'll never forget them. The water holes dry up in periods of drought, and they'd come to drink at the place where I lived. The impression of their power and their grace have never left me. The strangest thing was the contrast between their elegance and remarkable physical condition and the harsh, arid environment they were in. Australia has the largest population of wild horses in the world: more than a million. These animals are the progenies of horses brought over by the settlers that then escaped or were abandoned. They've adapted to every environmental condition: deserts, mountains, forests, coasts and even islands. Through natural selection they have developed an inexhaustible stamina. My romantic vision, however, was soon tarnished by the many people who consider these creatures an invasive species – a scourge.

I would soon discover that brumbies are descended from thoroughbreds and Arabian horses imported from South Africa and England in the eighteenth century. They're the offspring of those horses who would go on to accompany millions of Australian soldiers during wars fought alongside the British and Allied Forces. Whether it was the Boer War, or in World War I – at Gallipoli, in Palestine at Beersheba, or in France, where millions of horses were sent to every front – except a solitary one, none ever returned. They either died in combat or, for the survivors, repatriation to Australia was too expensive: all were victims of human ungratefulness. The advocates for the wild offspring of these horses stress their resilience and capacity to withstand any kind of environment. They're used today in all sorts of disciplines, including equine therapy, which helps people overcome a disability through connecting with horses. Brumbies are inquisitive and big-hearted. Once you have earned their trust, you will share a bond unlike anything you'd experience with a domestic horse.

Reading everything I could get my hands on, I learnt that their name is thought to have come from Sergeant James Brumby, a soldier and pastoralist who, one day in 1804, freed his horses when moving to Tasmania. Another possible origin for their moniker is '*baroomby*', which means 'wild' in the Pitjara language of Central Australia. The word 'brumby', referring to horses which have returned to the wild, was written down for the first time in 1880, in the *Australasian Magazine*, a Melbourne newspaper.

I felt a surge of instinctive defensiveness for the brumbies – considered to be pests by the Australian government. That's when the idea began to germinate in my mind. Why not devise a big adventure using brumbies for company, to perhaps promote a recognition of their uniqueness; not to save them all – from massacres like the one in Guy Fawkes River National Park in 2000, where some six hundred horses were culled with sniper rifles from a helicopter – but to at least participate in avoiding new massacres from taking place? The foundation of the Guy Fawkes Heritage Horse Association stemmed from the huge outrage these killings created in the media. The association's goal is to manage the brumby population numbers, while ensuring and promoting their historic, military and cultural value. Since then, aerial culling has been prohibited in New South Wales, and the association was able to register Guy Fawkes horses as a heritage breed.

Strangely, this all started for me when I was a youth worker in Ltyentye Apurte, an Arrernte Indigenous community, also known as Santa Teresa, in the Northern Territory, about 80 kilometres south-east of Alice Springs. Established in 1950 as a Catholic mission, it became home to people from Alice Springs as well as those from another mission in the former goldmining town of Arltunga. I was invited to participate in a horse race. I was the only female rider – and a white female rider, at that. I still remember the dusty, burning desert light when, to my and everyone else's surprise, I won the race, in front of a stunned all-male audience. Sometimes, I also think the seeds of this adventure were sown when, at the age of five, I had my first riding lesson, which would lead my younger sister and me to compete in eventing for the *École Militaire*, a local equestrian school. Then I wonder if it didn't begin when I first met my now ex-partner at a music festival in North Melbourne. Damian brought me to discover this country, this continent. Thanks to him I discovered the outback; its beauty, rawness and vastness blew me away. I chose to work with Aboriginal children who were bursting with life and intelligence. I would spend twelve years with them, on and off; twelve years in which I expended the best of my time, energy and imagination that I could. I was lucky to learn about their extraordinary culture, their traditions, their way of life and, more importantly, their unique understanding of nature and of being part of the universe.

Loneliness? There's no loneliness here. One is a piece of bark, a leaf, a snapping branch, a pool of sunlight. That red earth under the bare soles of one's feet. I'm never afraid of this environment, which never betrays me, even in the toughest times. I learn to skirt danger and melt in the bush. The trees, all these trees – these eucalypts – are friends, wise parents. A savage, scented belonging. In daily contact with Aboriginal people, I learn to face the most desperate situations, to be content with little and to always find a solution. Thanks to them I get to know the brumbies.

It's also from the Aboriginal community that I adopted my dog, Fox, a dingo mongrel, twelve years ago. He's my most precious friend. He has a tan coat, black nose and ears, and his fur is as long and soft as a border collie's. When I met Fox, he was a skinny, shy stray. I started feeding him and, three weeks later when our programme came to an end in that community, I told my partner of the time that I was going to adopt him. This did not go down well. I simply responded that *he* wasn't adopting the dog, *I* was. And I did. Looking back, I don't think I could have done the Trail without Fox. As much as I love my horses and have created a unique bond with them, they don't fit into my tent at night and they don't lick me to death when I'm down, trying to cheer me up.

Dingos are as wild as brumbies but they're native to Australia. At night you hear them howling like wolves, which can take some getting used to on your first night camping under the stars in a swag. The sound of their cries is one you never quite forget. Dingos, in their natural state, live in packs of about twelve – a dingo family. They're small wolves, indeed – very tough, with a soft fur, weighing between 10 and 20 kilograms, and very fast: they can reach peaks of 65 kilometres an hour. They breed only once a year but have litters of up to eight puppies. The Aboriginal community tells me that they can predict droughts this way – the larger the litters, the higher the risk of a dry season, because more pups equals a better chance of having survivors.

The brumbies' destiny gnawed at me; their fate triggered a subterranean feeling to which I responded viscerally. It became so important, more important than everyday goals, than long-term plans, than family expectations ... I was twenty-nine, but age, time, circumstance and place didn't have much to do with it ... After I had made the decision to cross the continent with three brumbies, on the Bicentennial National Trail, I stumbled upon Robyn Davidson's story – she crossed Australia from east to west with camels. If she did it, I felt I could have a shot at it, too. But to undertake the expedition, I needed money. So, I went back into the bush for a year, working as a social worker, and I saved up, a dollar at a time. Then, to toughen up, I decided to spend six months on Graeme and Erica's farm. I get up at 5am every morning, as the settlers probably had. I help Erica and Graeme with the farm work: looking after the animals, chopping wood, repairing the fences, tending the vegetable garden, and also working at a nearby potato farm. With them, I learn to train wild horses with a technique similar to natural horsemanship, a lot gentler than the traditional one. The aim of the technique is to get horses to accept both saddle and rider, to carry a pack saddle and to all travel together in harmony. The success behind Erica's method consists of adapting to each animal: 'Some feel an overwhelming fear, others don't. We try to give each one the opportunity of being tamed. It can take much more time with certain temperaments,' Erica explains.

I acquire my first brumby, Cooper, another buckskin gelding of four years, who fits all the requirements because he's so docile. Then Dokka and Guy, but I'm forced to give them up becauase of their intractable characters. After that comes River, a young palomino – a very popular breed in Western films of the sixties. He's only two, going on three, but he really catches my eye. His face is crooked but, to me, this gives his features character. Finally, Roxanne, my only mare: twelve years old, with a bay coat, like a good whiskey, and already trained. She diminishes my budget by $4000. There is no getting out of the expense, if I want to get my team ready on time.

Enduring and strong, Roxanne will reveal herself to be worth her weight in gold. I mainly choose colts, and geld them. I know that a mare can create havoc when encountering the herds of wild horses, whom I won't fail to meet on the Trail, but I stick to my choice. Relieved to have found my team, I now have three horses which I will be able to rotate in a reliable method. The packhorse will carry all my camping equipment, plus food rations, two first-aid kits – one for me and one for my horses – as well as solar panels. I will ride the second horse, while the last brumby will be at rest. I'll alternate my steed every day, a vital measure for my companions' survival on such a long trek. The pack saddle, a dead weight for the horse's back, can create friction and sores, and this will require regular attention.

Having never owned a horse, I learn all I can about their essential needs. Erica and a local vet help me put together a comprehensive first-aid kit for them. I will carry antibiotics and a suture kit and other essential medicines I might need to administer. Erica and Graeme also teach me the art of barefoot trimming. I decide not to shoe my horses to avoid carrying heavy shoeing gear. My intention is to get through these thousands of kilometres with the same horses from start to finish – a challenge nobody has ever pulled off, to my knowledge.

A wild horse must be taught every single thing in order to be prepared for unexpected events on the trek and to avoid disaster. I have to get my brumbies used to road traffic, because we'll encounter cars and trucks on the way;

to the hobbles, those straps that tether their front legs; to staying behind the electric tape circling the bivouac at night; to walking three abreast in harmony; to crossing all sorts of obstacles; and to remaining calm when facing any unexpected noise – all this, as Australians have told me, will make him or her bomb-proof.

The three months of training have morphed into six.

Erica, and her weathered, acid-proof spirit, teaches me the merit of a certain hardness to oneself and others. I'll be forever grateful to her for it – even if her toughness isn't always easy to cope with on an everyday level! With her partner, Graeme, Erica founded the Guy Fawkes Heritage Horse Association, successfully establishing a pragmatic, but humane, programme to manage the number of wild horses in the Guy Fawkes River National Park, following the 'passive' trapping method. This consists of luring the horses with food into panel yards, set up as traps, and then taking them out of the park. They sell the majority of the wild horses to the public, and the small percentage that are not suitable for domestic life to the slaughterhouse. This may seem cruel, but it's a much more humane method than aerial culling. I'm so indebted to Erica and Graeme's generous help and am truly grateful for their support. One of my goals throughout my Trail odyssey is to promote their association and to honour them by succeeding in my adventure – which they doubt I will achieve. But I want to show them how much their lessons stood me in good stead.

Exhausted, both morally and physically, I decide to go and see my family in France. I use the opportunity on the way to meet a well-known Danish horse trainer. After four days, and a bill of €1000, the man tells me that my project hasn't got a hope in hell. Anyway, he explains, women should have no business with horses. He obviously has no knowledge of Joan of Arc, Eleanor of Aquitaine, and Mary, Queen of Scots – to mention but three. But I'm going to need more than a misogynistic guru with a moneyed clientele to discourage me.

In Paris, where I was born, I take the time to gaze up at the quadriga on top of the Grand Palais museum, sculpted by Récipon. I've always wanted to follow those four horses taking flight over the roofs of Paris, and remember the day my Aunt Sylvie pointed them out to me, when I was a teenager.

On my return to Australia, I work on the training of my three friends. The equipment I need is expensive: navigation tools, first-aid kits, and good quality saddles that won't injure my companions. I read every detail about the twelve sections of the Trail. Each section presents a particular challenge: the south because of its isolation and the mountainous terrain of the Australian Alps, and the north because of its hot climate, its tropical storms and its crocodiles.

I'm aware of the spiders, crocodiles and twelve of the world's deadliest species of snakes inhabiting the Australian bush. I know that, after being bitten by one of these, you go into cardiac arrest within a few hours – and I'll be days away from any medical help. Even though I won't have any normal tools of communication, I will take an emergency device that includes a satellite phone. I'm also taking along a SPOT tracker, which is linked to a satellite. Pressing a button will give my position to Erica, who will be my expedition manager, and to my family. I will always wear it on my belt. It has three message buttons:

- I'm safe and sound and have reached my destination.
- I need help within 48 hours.
- I'm in mortal danger. Send a helicopter.

Money and food are priorities. I teach my three friends to get used to pellets, to which they're not accustomed, in anticipation of having to camp in places where grass cannot be found. These dietary supplements will become vital tools of survival. As far as I'm concerned, dehydrated food, normally used in this kind of expedition, is too expensive. I'll make do with couscous, pasta, rice, sardines, canned tuna, peas and porridge for a year, so as to limit the packhorse's burden, which must not be over 60 kilograms. I also need to vaccinate my horses against tetanus, typhoid and especially against the Hendra virus, which is present in Queensland. Transmitted by bats, it's deadly to both horses and humans.

I make a first test-outing with River, Cooper and Roxanne to make sure that I know how to use all the equipment and how to manage my horses. In the course of that first night, I realise what our lives will be like for a year. Liberated from every tie, off the grid, disconnected – I'm coming 'down off this feather-bed of civilisation', to quote Robert Louis Stevenson. Alone with nature and freed of the world's allure, I'll only be accountable to my horses. A frugal life of bare essentials in which time will slow down – the idea fills me with joy. Suddenly awed that I have made it up to this point, I prepare to venture into an unknown world full of mysterious tomorrows.

I still hardly have any sponsors. The logistics of the expedition is devouring my days. Season follows season, and time is running out. I've decided to leave from the south in November, before the cold weather kicks in. In the mountains, snow and rains would hamper our progress. All these efforts – all this research, all this training – are a challenge in themselves. But for me they are part and parcel of the adventure. It takes me a year and a half to get ready. You can't turn up on the Trail, one of the longest treks in the world, as if you were tripping down a country lane. Reginald Murray, 'RM' Williams, who first imagined the Trail, wanted it to compete with the Appalachian Trail, a hiking path of 3510 kilometres across the Appalachian Mountains on the east coast of the United States. RM Williams, who created such a well-known brand of clothing, started off as a swagman, and that, for me, is such an inspiration.

I had already been on a few expeditions in my early twenties with my ex, Damian. In Irkutsk, in Siberia, we bought a very old Ural sidecar motorbike, which we rode back to France over 10,000 kilometres, camping all the way. We started off with very little money and broke down dozens of times. The Russians always helped us out. In Mongolia, we rode horses across 900 kilometres, over three months at the end of winter 2007, camping in snowstorms at temperatures of

-20 degrees Celsius. This time I'm doing it alone for more than a year, and with the added enormous responsibility of keeping my horses in good condition. Perhaps that's what I'm following so doggedly: trying to reach hidden extremes that were not part of my European map.

At last, we're ready. We go down south. At the cost of a few more thousand dollars, we reach Healesville, Victoria, in a truck, leaving from Dorrigo, New South Wales. I'll never get used to the thousands of kilometres Australians travel at the drop of a hat. There are no hitches on this long trip. We camp on the edges of towns, and the horses deal calmly with this first leg of the trip. I'm filled in equal measure with apprehension and euphoria. The truck driver, Kris, has me laughing the whole way and reassures me. If each person I meet on the trek is like him, everything should go well. But one should never take anything for granted …

A scary twist to my story: after all my planning, I nearly kill Cooper by giving him hay mixed with soy, which he isn't used to, and which is way too rich for his gut. I spend the night with him, appalled by my negligence. Colic can be fatal for horses! Luckily Cooper is very tough and survives his cramps.

But dread takes over me. Every single detail I have to foresee in the pressure of these last days is dizzying. We're so close to our departure, set for the 17th of November 2015.

Bending my rule of making the journey alone, I decide to gather a support team for the first month of the trek. The initial section, Section 12, if you choose to start from the south, is by far the most perilous: steep and isolated, it's particularly difficult for horses unacquainted with mountain terrain.

2

Starting Tough

Section 12: Healesville to Omeo

426 kilometres

17 November 2015 to 4 January 2016

D-day. I crawl out of my sleeping bag. We'd set up camp in a shed. It's still dark and I've hardly slept. The air is fresh. I stare at the sunrise in disbelief. It's so madly beautiful, it fills me with hope. I check my gear and the food rations for the umpteenth time. The weight must be perfectly balanced on the pack saddle before it's loaded onto Roxanne. The local press and a small group of onlookers surround us. I can feel my heart sinking at the idea of being separated from my dog, Fox. But we have to obey the rules of the Trail – no dogs in national parks – and that section in Victoria is mostly all parkland. Tenderly, I prepare my horses, patting them, whispering to them. The first hitch in this big challenge: the friend who had proposed logistic support with her four-wheel drive for a month decided at the last minute to ride with me, and has asked someone else to drive the backup vehicle instead. The horse she's just bought is not trained for the job. Rather than being a help, she's complicating things for me before we've even set off. Well, I've no other alternative.

Finally, we're in the saddle, moving towards the sign that indicates the beginning of the horse trail. I touch the stone bearing Dan Seymour's plaque – this man lead the inaugural BNT journey in the early seventies with his two horses and his dog. Sponsored by RM Williams, who had become a patron, the Trail was conceived to link all the different stock routes. To this day thirty-seven people have managed to complete the Trail – some on foot, some on a bicycle, some on horseback, changing horses on the way. Up to now, only one woman has completed it alone, riding horses. No-one has done it with three wild ones.

After a year and a half of intensive preparation, it's a strange, exhilarating experience to see my dream taking shape in the real world. *Are my horses and I ready for this crazy expedition?* I ask myself, as we slowly blend into a forest of giant eucalypts and lush ferns – simmering with life. We hear all kinds of insects, and an orchestra of kookaburras, parrots and lyrebirds. A few wallabies hop across our path. For this very first day, I have chosen to ride Cooper. Roxanne is the packhorse, and River, the youngest, whom I want to spare, is at rest. I've planned to ride 20 to 40 kilometres a day.

My brumbies follow, and are adapting rather well to the gradually rising path. My friend's horse, on the other hand, is very nervous. The four-wheel drive has trouble following us, and flounders on this nearly unmarked rugged four-wheel track. For me, the vehicle is vital. It's transporting horse feed for this gruelling section, and dozens of litres of water, which would be too heavy for my horses to carry. The backup vehicle is meant to transport most of the equipment, so the weight on the packhorse can be increased gradually, as the horses grow accustomed to sharing this daily task. I've been warned that water could be scarce in the following days, when I reach the top of the mountains – and a horse downs 20 litres of water per day.

The first bivouac night is with a fire, and an electric fence fed by a solar panel for my horses. Their forelegs are hobbled with two leather bracelets linked by chain, and sometimes a side hobble, too, which is attached to a posterior leg. But my friend's horse worries us until morning. Her last-minute disruption is driving me nuts. How could she imagine riding with me on a whim, when my horses and I have been preparing ourselves for months?

As we rise in altitude, the horizons rise in majesty. The rivers we cross and the grasses we tread are nearly too clear and deeply green to be true. We've been gone for only four days but my companions are starting to feel the kilometres in their legs. River, the youngest, seems to prefer lolling in the grass rather than eating it. We reach the first shelter, Keppel Hut. The shack – freshly rebuilt after being destroyed in bushfires, the first dating from 1983 – is a welcome surprise. Farmers stayed here when they were mustering their cattle to their summer pastures. The night is pretty cold.

After a week, the nights grow even colder as the mountains loom closer. Our team hasn't quite hit its stride and the ground is becoming steeper and steeper. My horses are balking, and my friend is no help at all. And, this evening, by the campfire, she announces that she's leaving us.

I'm torn between relief and the niggling worry of facing alone one of the most challenging sections of the Trail – Butcher Country. The aptly named 1325-metre-high Mount Terrible is part of it. I'm concerned about travelling across mountain peaks where water is rare and weather unpredictable.

That same night, while lost in thought gathering wood, luck looks my way. Just as I'm wondering how I'm going to cover this precipitous terrain, a man and his horses materialise from the surrounding trees. Like me, he has one packhorse and rides another. His chestnut geldings are Tennessee Walkers, a breed from the US developed to be a comfortable and hardy horse, capable of travelling great distances. The rider, dressed in a long Driza-Bone and a dog-eared cowboy hat – its stains and holes bearing witness to all it's been through – is in his sixties. Gentle-eyed, and rough around the edges, he's coming towards us. Swallowing half his words, in the Australian way, he greets us. His name is Finnie. I invite him to set up camp near us, but ask him to keep his horses apart from ours. Sitting around the fire, we chat. I share my dilemma with him. This guy I've only just met proves himself to be a lover and horse-riding encyclopedia of the Trail. He proposes to take his horses back home the very next day and then meet me as soon as possible with his four-wheel drive. His decision to help me through the hostile territory to come is taken in the spur of the moment.

Early in the morning, I get ready to leave – alone this time. Finnie and my friend have left me. I no longer have the four-wheel drive's support. We only left eight days ago, and, for the first time, my horses must bear all the equipment and three weeks' worth of food rations. To put the cherry on the cake, the sun has given up the ghost and a solid drizzle sets in. I'm more worried about my ability to manage the animals, and the search for water and resources, than about loneliness. The next four days test our stamina, and the night we reach the designated camping site in the Trail guide we're in a dark forest. There isn't a blade of grass for the horses; there is only dead trunks littering the dry earth. My companions will rest on an empty stomach – with no backup vehicle, there's no pellets. I'm ashamed to eat in front of them. We've done so many kilometres through trying ground already, and the next waterhole is too far to reach before night.

The next morning, I'm appalled when I realise how much time I need to pack all our gear after breakfast. Between preparing the horses and allocating the equipment, three hours go by before we can set off. I suddenly wonder if I'm not setting about this the wrong way. By the end of the day, as luck has it, a reward greets us. I find a place to stop along a river with thick, luscious, tasty grass for Roxanne, River and Cooper. It's a struggle against time – a strong wind has picked up. I choose my camp near the water deliberately, setting up my tent away from the trees. The river and its flowing current are a welcome opportunity for me to wash myself. I'm longing to keep clean. The water rushes over the stones, along with my worries.

After taking care of the horses, I hobble them, so they can graze on the lovely grass, which they missed out on the night before. The Big River, full of tranquil waterholes, runs peacefully through a state forest. I'm cooking over my fire, which burns bright with the branches I have scavenged, when a fisherman appears in his four-wheel drive. In his sixties, he has a warm expression peeping out from under his beanie hat, and a slight silhouette. He tells me his name is Bill and warns me about the weather forecast: an approaching storm with winds of 130 kilometres an hour. He's concerned about us. I reassure him. The horses, formerly wild, have been through worse. All night, the wind howls, and we're surrounded by the eerie sound of creaking branches and falling trees. The skies seem to be ripping themselves apart. At one point, my tent, though securely tethered, is suddenly slammed to the ground as if by a gigantic hand. I go out into the gale to check on the horses several times during the night. They're standing strong in the face of it all.

At daybreak, I discover the extent of the damage: dozens of trees have been torn down by the storm. I decide to take a good day's rest to allow my companions to enjoy the high-quality grass around here. Bill returns – he's still worried about me. He tells me about the campers a few kilometres from here who ended up in hospital when their tent was hit by falling trees. Then he goes off fishing again; the woods and the river are his home. At the end of the day, he returns with a gift – a rainbow trout. I'm so happy to eat something so fresh and delicate, and cook it on glowing embers. What a treat …

The next day, we get ready for the climb up Mount Terrible. Three hours of preparation are again necessary before setting off. We climb, and climb, and climb, painstakingly. Soon, the forest ground drops away, far below. Cooper keeps pulling back, testing my patience. I walk alongside the horses to relieve them, but each of Cooper's tugs nearly yanks my arm off. The ground is rocky and abrupt, and we're impeded by trees that were felled by the storm, sometimes having to wend our way around, over or under the trunks littering our path.

We reach the foothills of the Australian Alps. Even if the mornings are cool, the sun beats down on us all through the day. As the slopes become more precipitous, my companions find it difficult to walk in sync. One or the other of the geldings is always lagging behind, slowing our progress, and I have to pull him up. Roxanne, my mare, staunchly at my side, takes the lead. I thank my lucky stars she's with me.

Swearing like a trooper, sweating profusely, I reach the summit of Mount Terrible. My steeds are dripping, and the geldings seem to be wondering why I'm putting them through this misery. I look at Cooper and tell him he's stronger and braver than he thinks; he must stop being such a sook. The people who've imagined this trek are sadists, I tell myself. Why take a horse into such places, at such heights? Twenty times during the ascent, I ask myself what I'm doing here. I'm so focused on the incredible efforts that such a trek imposes on us that I'm incapable of hearing the birds or looking at anything else but the path in front of me. Two attributes of these mountains, loose stones and scree, dog our pilgrims' progress. In 1988, an old Trail coordinator, Ian Taylor, admitted that some portions of the Trail were unbelievably harsh, adding: 'We wanted the users of the Trail to feel a little of what a settler's life had been.' Well, they've succeeded.

The following days are not much more encouraging; the summits are as gruelling as those of Mount Terrible. Giddying descents, which are even harder on the horses, come in rapid succession, Cooper and River using their legs as breaks as much as they can. The region is also infested with snakes – I see them on our path. I scan the track ahead to safeguard the horses from being bitten. When I spot a tiger snake taking a nap on the narrow track, and it refuses to skedaddle when I throw stones at him – the usual way to make them flee – we are forced to make a detour through the trees on the slope.

For a few days, we travel through areas that have been ravaged by bushfires. In February 2009, thousands of hectares of trees burned up in the Black Saturday bushfires. The surviving black-and-grey trunks are like ghosts – the dead souls of this cemetery I must cross. It's daytime in summer, and the tops of these mountains are a furnace. My jeans are too warm – I sometimes take them off and walk in just my underwear and boots. The only ones who can see me and laugh are my horses. When we reach the top of a mountain, we enjoy a smoky, blue ridgeline torn up by shreds of mist. But this respite is of short duration. Far, far in the distance, through a gap in the trees, with its entourage of climbs and drops, one can make out the next peak.

The ascent of Lazarini Spur is the most harrowing. A landscape of sinuous paths, its vegetation of dense trees is such that, from the sky, it must seem like a carpet. For two weeks now, I have been on foot, pulling River or Cooper up these steep climbs and down these abrupt descents. I start swearing, and set River free. 'Go,' I tell him, 'do what you want. I'm sick of dragging you along.' Letting him go is a sign of total despair. I have no idea if he'll follow us. When one of the horses starts pulling on a downward slope, it makes the whole experience extremely hard for all of us. I, for one, am spreadeagled between the one behind and those pulling ahead – each of us in a precarious position. So, exhausted, I set him loose, restore him to freedom, and continue on with

Roxanne and Cooper, petrified at the idea that River will not follow. His feet are visibly hurting him on this mountainous terrain, but after a few minutes on his own, picking his way along, he gently joins us. Relieved, I keep on like this until we reach our camp.

That night, we've only travelled 15 kilometres and we arrive much too late to set up a bivouac. I'm wrecked – my whole body is hurting, and I'm bruised from head to toe from falling over on the rocky ground. I don't know how I'll find the strength to put up my tent or to fence off an area for the horses. I sleep as if I've fallen into a well.

Night does its silent work, and the next morning I'm ready to go. I have been getting used to the idea that it takes us time to get ready. I rise earlier and earlier. Yet, after another ascent with Cooper and River being as uncooperative as ever, I lose it. I throw the reins on the ground, dripping with sweat and exhausted from bracing myself while pulling the two geldings along as I walk at their sides. I squat down in tears and ask myself seriously if I'm going to manage 5000 kilometres with these two obstinate mules. Suddenly, I spring to my feet in agony. I have been crouching on a nest of jack jumper ants, and they've stung my bum. Nature has forced me to get back on my feet, reminding me that there's a battle to be fought and that it's no use whinging.

I'm ashamed of my tears. I look at Roxanne and talk to her, begging her to help me.

An idea comes to me for a new system that I hope will help us in our ascent. I pass a leather hobble strap around Roxanne's neck and attach the two geldings to her, so she can pull them up.

This new method starts to yield results, but it's dicey on steep paths. If one of the horses loses their footing, the others will be dragged down, too. I myself often slip in the descents. But we're starting to form a team thanks to this system, which brings them to understand that they can't opt out of their fair share of the work. From now on, Cooper and River climb the slopes more vigorously, strengthened by their intestinal fortitude.

Habits set in. Up early, we're on the move till the mid-afternoon. I don't stop for lunch, so as to avoid keeping my companions standing with weight on their backs. At the end of each leg, I look after them first. It's a rule I never bend. I relieve the pack horse of his or her saddle, which is the heaviest. I wash them and check them over for any wounds, and then I hobble them so they can graze. I go to bed early.

Water, grass, and shade are my three priorities in choosing where to set up my bivouac. Every day, I create an ephemeral home in the bush. Dependent on the wind, I choose where to build my campfire, surrounding it with river stones. I erect my tent, and lay out my saddle gear to dry off the sweat. The sheepskin I sleep on is also my armchair in front of the fire. At sundown, I unravel the electric tape that will serve as my horses' enclosure for the night – always positioned close by me so I can hear them. I study the following day's navigation plan. The guide's survey is not always precise or up to date. To add an additional difficulty, the Trail was conceived in twelve sections from north to south, but because I started from the south I must read it upside-down – and the directions can get absurd. Another golden rule: I must never leave behind any trace of my presence.

After a trying day – still in the Lazarini Spur section – when approaching the planned camping spot, I hear bells. I move closer and meet a couple of Australians, Kathryn and Preston, with their horses. In her thirties, she's brown haired, blue eyed, with a gentle face. He's a darker blond, a little older, with a few days' stubble and a benign expression. They're riding down the Trail, towards the south, at bookends with me. Water is quite far away, and we help each other out in retrieving it. It's so nice to meet them, and they're so friendly. They started on the Trail fifteen months ago and have 5000 kilometres under their belts, while I have a puny two hundred from two weeks' riding.

I'm full of admiration for the good physical condition of their five horses. I like hearing the cowbells that hang around their steeds' necks. Perfectly organised, hampered by very little equipment, they've accumulated a fount of knowledge about the horses and the lay of the land, and they share this wealth of information with me. In return, I give them precision detail on what they'll be riding into. Preston has talent as a farrier; he has furnished his five horses with boots, and horseshoes in very light aluminium. I ask him to check my brumbies' feet. He assures me they're still in good nick, but tells me they won't be able to stay that way for thousands of kilometres. They'll need horseshoes or boots. This worries me, because I'm about three weeks from the first local community. Thanks to Preston and Kathryn, I learn that copra, dried coconut albumen, mixed with water, can be used as a dietary supplement for the horses. This powder, very light to carry, expands in contact with water. The next day, I say goodbye to the benevolent duo and tell them how grateful I am. They give me my first horse bell and warn me that the next tracks scale terrible peaks and that I will find myself very isolated.

Two days later, sitting resting in a field on the bank of Macalister River, I see a white Land Cruiser pick-up driving towards me. It's Finnie – all battered cowboy hat, gap-toothed smile and deceptively vacant blue-eyed gaze – who has managed to find us in this steep, craggy landscape. I'm awe-struck and so happy to see him. The man has found his way, without any means of communication, following my horses' footprints like a tracker. I'm relieved, too – I know his help will be so precious, two days from crossing the famous Butcher Country, known for its lack of water and feed. Finnie has brought up lots of fresh produce, and his favourites 'froffies' (beers). Ever the bushman, limping on his bowlegs because of a bad knee, he cooks me a delicious lunch on his fire, which renews me physically and morally.

We check out the next few days' navigation together, and, suddenly, while we're each absorbed in our daily tasks, a large, white, four-wheel drive Land Cruiser looms up, charging straight at us. It stops, and three sinister-looking men climb out, dressed in military fatigues, armed to the teeth – daggers, ammunition belts, boot knives – and holding a growling, drooling pit bull, straining on his leash. These men, probably hunters, between forty and fifty, don't look Australian. One of them is wearing yellow aviator sunglasses that make him look like he's from another time. They prowl arrogantly around our camp, before addressing us with their heavy Eastern European accents. Then they start talking between themselves, but we can't understand a single word. They have large dead snakes and a dingo on the roof of their four-wheel drive. Blood drips from the car, and they boast of shooting at anything that moves. Finnie and I feign the utmost calm. Presumably, they're trying to intimidate us. Then they ask us questions. Wary, we keep our answers as vague as we can, and I avoid alluding to my solo trek. Neither of us has any difficulty imagining their dark intentions. After a 20 minute discussion that feels like a century, they finally depart. That night, locked in my tent with my knife under my pillow, I don't sleep a wink, terrified at the idea of them returning. Finnie spends his night in the back of his pick-up, his rifle at hand's reach.

At daybreak, we tackle the Butcher Country ascent. For this trek, I set off on foot with my horses, and Finnie goes ahead of us in his four-wheel drive to assess the terrain. His vehicle is having a hard time; the incline is so steep and the washouts so great that the track has had to be levelled out every 20 metres to facilitate passage. Finnie waits for me every few kilometres, with his usual kindness. I arrive scarlet-faced, panting, my horses shrouded in misty clouds of sweat, and we take a break to give us time to catch our breath. Finnie offers a cool drink. The higher we rise, the more the landscape changes. The grass, scarcer now, is only snowgrass, burnt by the snow which covers it for the main part of the year.

We haven't gotten through many kilometres, but Finnie's presence allows us to bivouac where we fancy, because he has water and food for the horses. He notices that his four-wheel drive's coil springs are damaged. At the end of the afternoon, in the dying light, we share a few 'froffies' and enjoy the escarpments, the blue, misty peaks, unravelling the immensity of Australia before us. In the dry dusk air, eagles, rulers of this land, pierce the silence with their strident calls. I love the baroque shapes that the clouds form in the setting sun. We discuss possible scenarios. He envisages, if his four-wheel drive can't make it to the next leg, continuing with me on one of my horses.

That night, it rains. When we wake up in the morning, the world is wrapped in a dense fog. But the clock is still ticking, and we have a long day ahead of us in which to reach a shelter called Howitt Hut.

We set off, and Finnie leaves, keen to test his vehicle. I walk slowly with my horses in the pouring rain, which obstructs our vision. A strong blizzard rises, blowing straight at us. It bothers the horses, who walk with their heads sideways. A horse has no front vision and can only see from the sides. My head is bent, with my Driza-Bone coat reaching to my feet. With my cowboy hat, riding alone in the mountains, I feel like the 'man from Snowy River.' Isn't the poem about brumbies, after all? I'm hoping I'll be as successful on these steep slopes as he was.

Drenched to the bone and hardly able to see my way, I'm relieved to catch a glimpse of the humble mountain shelter. At 1545 metres, it was built around the start of the twentieth century. It's one of the highest shelters in Victoria. In this rudimentary shack, you find cut wood, a few tin cans of food, matches and a stone fireplace: the bare essentials for survival. Around the fire, I dry my equipment and my clothes. Finnie and I drink a few 'froffies', happy to be under a roof in this storm. 'Love, you've been kissed on the ass by an angel,' he tells me. I fall into a deep sleep on the wooden sleeping platform.

Next morning, I wake up at the sound of the bell I've hung around Roxanne's neck to a perfect blue sky. I've made myself a new friend, a red robin or *miro boodang*, perched on the windowsill, bold as brass. I step out of the hut, stunned by the view. Snow gums, wildflowers and yellow gentians frame the plateau. Clouds of butterflies patrol the pastures of snowgrass. The peaks of Mount Howitt, Bogong and Feathertop claim the distant horizon. Finnie is leaving us. He's going home. I decide to linger and enjoy this mesmerising place. Roxanne,

River and Cooper play in a paddock, which is already fenced for cattle. They're having a field day, rearing and kicking under the sky in pure enjoyment.

When I leave Howitt Plains Hut, the Trail morphs into a single mountain path plunging down into Wonnangatta Valley, becoming so narrow that you have to search for it all the way. Till now the horses could walk three abreast, but here it's impossible. I have to dismount to guide the horses, meandering between the trees, which is quite a feat. Cooper, the laziest, keeps getting on my nerves. Instead of following in single file, he follows his own agenda, and almost has us all tumbling down to the bottom of the valley below. When I'm already having a difficult time with the packhorse, who has a wider load, Cooper keeps on going on the wrong side of trees, dragging us backwards.

This descent is hard work but mentally gratifying. The views that greet me at every turn seem to insist that everything is worth it. In this extreme wilderness, Wonnangatta Valley is very wide, its flanks covered with yellowed grass and enormous dark-green trees. The trees stand, alive with beauty, handing me their stunning reward in answer to all my efforts. I see a few stone ruins, vestiges of the first settlers and of the gold-diggers of the last years of the 1860s.

On our way up again, since the Trail evolves from valleys

into peaks, we find ourselves bereft of water. Coerced into travelling additional kilometres in search of an alternative, we must make do with a pretty nauseating greenish pond. I have water purifying pills, but this is beyond any purifying ... As fate has it, I meet a cyclist who, between periods of work, has been following sections of the Trail for a couple of years. He's the definition of the lightweight, rugged traveller. He has very little gear on his bike. Soap and toothbrush are definitely absent from his kit's bare essentials, and his hair appears to host a nest of unwanted guests. He explains that I was lucky in the high Victorian country, because its streams are so pristine, but I should have a water filter. In spite of his oddities, he's friendly and I enjoy his company. We filter enough water for the night and the next day. Without him I would have had to make do with half a litre of drinking water till the next day's camp. (*Kissed by an angel again*, I think to myself.)

I continue my progression in this wild area, with its abrupt slopes – so tough to handle. Before the descents, I adjust the pack saddle's harness. If it slips towards the horse's neck, it could create a wound. On the plateau, I stumble upon a group of four-wheel drive enthusiasts – a television crew. They're filming a documentary on the most adventuresome treks in Australia. The producer asks me, rather arrogantly, to get out of the way on a steep path. I refuse. I was there before him. Finally, he decides not to use it, judging it to be too risky. My horses and I handle it without too much trouble, and most importantly without incident. There's a certain satisfaction in this.

One evening, a while later, when camping on high ground in the middle of summer, a freezing cold descends and it starts snowing. My horses, with their short, summer coats, are not equipped for such weather. A thin layer of snow freezes my companions to the bone. They shake all night, and I have no rugs to offer them. Roxanne's shaking is the worst; I cover her with a synthetic tarp normally used to protect my equipment. In the days following, Cooper and River develop pulmonary infections. A yellow excretion oozes from their nostrils. They cough. I draw some antibiotics from my veterinary kit, which I inject into their necks twice a day. It's an intramuscular injection, with a long needle. I carefully change sides every time. It must be painful, but they seem to bear it very well.

Luckily, we're approaching a small town, Omeo, where new treatment will be available – and a few days' rest. That night, I hear rustling in the saddlebags and go out to discover that a family of water rats has disposed of our food rations. In the morning, I discover that they've even gnawed the saddlebags' leather itself. Damning them, the next day I hang our victuals to a tree.

We left on 17th of November, and we are a week away from Omeo – the only township in Section 12 of the BNT. I had given myself this objective to reach by Christmas. I arrive in this small town on the 22nd of December, which is at 685-metres altitude and counts only 400 souls. After living in the bush cut-off from everything for six weeks, even this meeting with 'society' causes a trance-like shock. Showing-off a tad, I choose to ride down the main street with my three horses on the way to the pub, and I'm irresistibly reminded of the Westerns I used to enjoy with my father as a kid. But the sound of my horses' hooves triggers a memory of the echo of hooves on the cobblestones of a village in France. In my late teens, I took a herd of horses up the Ardèche. Even a line of Victor Hugo's poem springs to mind: 'To hear your hooves, ringing on the ceiling of dreams'.

The owner of the pub offers me one of his paddocks to house my brumbies and my tent in. The inhabitants of Omeo are welcoming, as people often are in rural areas. At the pub, I meet old locals, real cowboys always ready to share a beer while relating stories from their youths as drovers. Their faces are weathered by the sun and by their harsh lives. Pot-bellied because of their beer-loving tendencies, the locals' tales reveal a part of the country's history – of the settlers, when life was tough and wild. I like their drawl. Some of these men are amusing, others are poignant.

This small locality was renowned in the 1850s during the goldrush, and its population went up to nine thousand. Even if today Omeo can only boast a very small population, its few beautiful colonial buildings still stand, like disproportionate giants, as witnesses of its past. The town's name, Omeo, means 'mountain' in the Aboriginal language. This is where I want to spend Christmas – an ideal opportunity for my brumbies to recover and for me to reorganise my equipment, to have some repairs done, as well as for me to prepare the logistics of the following weeks in the bush. I'm hunting everywhere for some boots to protect my companions' hooves. Kathryn and Preston were adamant that my horses' feet couldn't make the five-thousand-plus kilometres without them. I have sometimes resorted to using anti-inflammatories for their aching hooves, but it's not something I want to do long-term. I can't find a vet anywhere in the town, so I ask a local. He agrees to look at them out of the kindness of his heart and helps me in my search for boots. Besides, River and Cooper haven't completely recovered from their coughs. Before returning to the bush, I must check with my vet over the phone to see if he can send me extra medication. Luckily, there's a post office!

Omeo was known as the toughest and wildest township in this part of Australia. In this place, where so little services and shops are available, the inhabitants of the bush are used to being autonomous like everyone else in these remote rural areas – are able to handle all sorts of repairs and do leatherwork in their back sheds. In the garage of a friendly local, I get my rat-nibbled saddlebags repaired. I meet there an extraordinary half-Russian-half-Rumanian man, who lived in New Zealand and married an Englishwoman. The couple have settled in a nearby farm, have Guy Fawkes River National Park brumbies themselves, and they invite me to spend Christmas Eve with them. I'm stunned to encounter other people who are as passionate about these versatile horses as I am. She even competes in archery competitions on her brumby.

I abandon some of my heavier equipment – I've got to relieve my mounts of every possible ounce. I unstrap my cumbersome satellite telephone, which I've hardly used, having mainly relied on my SPOT tracker. I've already let go of my swag, and I've abandoned my large, sophisticated camera – too complicated to use when managing three horses, anyway.

This township marks the end of Section 12. The saying that those on the trail often share, 'Victoria makes you or breaks you!', fits the bill. We've got through this difficult stretch, and we've pulled it off.

In the pub, on Christmas day, a tall Christmas tree reigns in the dining room. Beer flows freely, children run around in circles of joy; Australian traditions are respected. Everyone seems to have adopted me, even if my adventure leaves many of the slightly misogynistic bushmen sceptical.

3

Beauties and Perils

Section 11: Omeo to Kosciuszko

201 kilometres

4 January to 28 January 2016

I start 2016 by retrieving my dog, Fox. I feel I could go to the end of the world in his loving, stalwart and reassuring company and am up to tackling the second leg of my journey, with a new frame of mind. Section 11 of the Trail will see us cross the first frontier leading into New South Wales. In spite of improved travelling conditions, I find no respite. Obsessed with their physical condition, I need to thoroughly monitor my horses. Friction against their backs must be avoided at all costs. Even the slightest sore near where the saddle sits takes weeks to heal. Their feet, one of their most vulnerable points, worry me constantly: 'No foot, no horse', the saying warns – and when a horse wounds him or herself on rocky terrain, a hoof abscess can happen all too quickly.

The need to find water and grass every day is another agonising issue. It's my honour-bound duty to know the lie of the land beforehand. Unlike cows, a horse is not a ruminant but a herbivore. He or she stocks very little food and so must eat continuously – for about 70 per cent of a twenty-four-hour day. For my horses, as Preston and Kathryn suggested, I always try to have a bit of copra to give them as a reward at the end of the day. A recurring difficulty is the weight inflicted on the packhorse – am I overloading them, or not? It's a delicate decision. For myself, I must also have enough food till the next supply point. Corresponding with the length of the segment, I post food parcels to myself to pick up at the cattle stations along the way. The Trail – not quite the country stroll – remains implacable.

When there's enough network coverage, another imperative is to try to call the station owners both to warn and thank them in advance while also giving them the approximate date and time of our passage through, so I can make sure the gates won't be locked. Some of the stations on the Trail cover hundreds of thousands of hectares. In North Queensland, the acreage is sometimes beyond a million hectares – as big as several French *départments*. The 'bush telegraph' also works well a lot of the time: one farmer warns the next one, and so on. People are usually expecting me or my call. I'm already breaking the rules with Fox, so it's imperative for me to nurture a good reputation on the Trail. I'm eager to demonstrate to those people who are generous enough to keep the Trail alive and allow strangers on their property that they're dealing with a trustworthy and respectful person.

Two days after leaving Omeo, I travel through Bindi Station, one of the most historic farms in Victoria. A sheep farm established in 1887, it spans 80 kilometres, and produces good wool. I visit the shearing shed. Shearing is a big operation at the station, taking place once a year and employing up to a hundred people. A seasoned shearer will shear a sheep in one minute – an incredible performance.

When it rains, I appreciate being allowed to sleep in a shed reserved for the staff. By candlelight, I stumble on the guest book with the signatures of the rare riders who have managed to accomplish a part or all of the chaotic tracks on the Trail. I read edifying tales, some up to twenty years old. One of them quotes Shakespeare's well-known 'Life's but a walking shadow …' As I hear the rain's patter on the corrugated iron roof above my head, these tales remind me of Baudelaire's poem 'The Voyage'. Are those forgotten Australian riders not indeed

'Astounding travellers ... What histories we read into your eyes, deeper than the ocean there. Show us the treasures of your rich memories, astounding jewels made of stars and air'?

In Omeo, I organise for some horse boots to be sent to me, which I learn to fit onto my companions' hooves to protect them from the unforgiving granitic terrain. After a few days' wear, they create sores on the horses' fetlocks. In fact, nothing is designed to be used for such distances. After travelling all day along the mountain peaks, the view is so breathtaking at this altitude that I stop on a promontory from where the land unveils itself for 360 degrees. I'm taking a risk, but the weather is mild, and the view of such bewildering beauty that I can't help myself. Mountains, covered with eucalypt forests, venture forth into infinity, where they merge into a blue halo. The leaves scenting the air are the mundane explanation for this halo. Baudelaire's 'Invitation to the Voyage' seems to be made for this view. 'There, there's only order, beauty: abundant, calm voluptuous.'

I gather some wood for the fire before preparing my meal of couscous. As I go about my business, I keep an ear out for the slightest sound of the horses' bells – I acquired two more in Omeo. While my dinner is simmering, I unravel my electric tape between the trees and attach the small solar panel to it, which never leaves my side. I'm lucky – my brumbies are scared stiff of this enclosure and, at least till now, haven't tried to go walkabout.

Roxanne, Cooper and River are settling into the rhythm of our nomadic life. As soon as we stop, they start grazing with gusto. They do the same when we find water along the way. No opportunity is wasted. Ragged clouds stream along the opalescent pink sunset. It's a joy to get undressed in Nature's palace. Our planet is so beautiful. One evening, I feel in such harmony with it all that instead of going to bed early, as usual, I wait for starlight. Under the Milky Way, which is unearthly in the Australian bush, you feel bathed in immensity and – however small – at one with it.

That night, from afar, I hear wild dogs howling. They sound like wolves. The Omeo farmers had warned me against these ferocious animals that attack their cattle. Descended from dingos – crossbred, often with strays from pig-hunting breeds – farmers shoot them and then hang them to their fences. I've seen some pretty enormous specimens. These howls leave the world bereft; they're an opportunity for loneliness to set in. I know I have long periods ahead where I will not meet a living human soul, where days will thread into each other, where my companions' footsteps will be my only rhythm and the wild sounds of the bush my only company. Then, the few people I meet on the way will flare up and acquire enormous stature in this flow, which could engulf me. Preceding trips have taught me this. Suddenly isolation can be a living bereavement. I won't feel lonely all the time but, when I least expect it, loneliness will come upon me; it will pounce without warning and there will be no respite.

Our next bivouac in the Trail guide is called Brumby Hill. There, I dread that my own dear horses' brethren may come and upset us during the night, since we're on their territory. Roxanne, the only mare, can be attractive to stallions: she's the one I'm most worried about. Twelve years old, captured at three, she was given the lengthiest training, understands more readily what I ask of her and does not change her rhythm during the course of the day. But she's a mare, she has spirit, and I must use sensitivity to solicit her. River, captured in 2015, a few months before our departure, is only two-and-a-half years old. He's had less time to adapt to men and domestic life and is the wildest in his thinking. He belongs more to his kind than to humans. Paradoxically, his temperament is very gentle; he likes me to tenderly caress his eye. Intelligent, he learns fast. Cooper was my first brumby, caught and adopted in 2014. I have a strong connection with him. He's the only one that I have entirely trained without outside help. I've managed to gain his trust. Together, we could go to the ends of the earth, despite him being the laziest of the three. A wild horse's life is not always easy – each day, as I ensured he was fed, his trust in me grew. He knows I will protect him.

On a warm afternoon, as I'm getting ready to choose my camp location near a stream, I notice hoof prints near the water. At all costs, I must avoid setting up my companions' electric enclosure anywhere near where wild horses usually water themselves. They do this at dusk and dawn – times when I must be particularly alert. As soon as I relieve the horses of their gear, I feel how tense they are. They sense something strange in their surroundings. Cooper, his ears pricked and his eyes peeled, is on the alert. Looking in the direction his ears are pointing towards, I see the silhouette of a horse behind the bushes. Roxanne and River, staring in that direction, have also seen him. Some thirty metres away, I see a magnificent paint stallion with a black-and-white coat. He surges from the bushes at a proud trot, a sure sign that we're on his territory. For kilometres now, I've sensed the presence of wild horses, sighting small mounds of dung, which stallions always leave in the same location to mark their territory.

River and Cooper become more and more nervous and tug at their tethers and halters. They're remembering their wild days – the outrage at such an encounter. The meeting of two stallions always involves a territorial conflict over herd or habitat. Cooper begins snorting, an alerting grunt indicating that he feels threatened. Now, other horses show themselves. The stallion has a few mares and their young. The hobbles on my poor brumbies aren't a very foolproof measure; it slows them down but doesn't stop them from galloping off. For more security, I tie the lead rope of their halter to a tree and go about organising my camp noisily, to keep the intruders at a distance. I set up the horse enclosure in the most rational way possible and erect my tent inside it so that I will be as close to them as possible. I can't leave them to spend the whole night tied to a tree unable to graze …The next day, I depart very early to shorten the 'torment of Tantalus'. I end the day's travels mid-afternoon, hobbling the back and front legs of my valiant steeds, leaving their halters and tethers on. I must prevent them from giving in to the call of the wild. Once the wild horses are out of sight, I let my companions graze to their hearts' content. I spend the night listening to every one of their movements. Cooper's snorting signals any foreign presence. I get up regularly to make noises and flash my torch, hoping to dissuade other brumbies from coming nearer.

My first encounters with wild horses on the Trail have been stunning. It's a mesmerising spectacle seeing these animals in their natural state. The freedom in their movements has something majestic about it. But such a confrontation is also nerve-racking, representing a real danger, a real threat for my companions. In this section, stories abound of riders losing their mounts; of their mounts running off with passing brumbies. But, for me, the episode ends without mishap – I have been prepared. The detection of hoof prints, piles of dung, and the warning noises emanating from my horses helped us cope.

We deal with continuous rain for the next few days, and we'll soon be crossing the Murray River, one of the longest rivers in Australia, a natural frontier between Victoria and New South Wales. Other encounters with brumbies take place; we're on their territory. Some are painful, like on the day my horses prick up their ears, and I see, a few steps in front of us, a dead mare lying on the track. I've already heard of certain methods of capture practised by a cynical group of locals, the 'brumby runners', who think they're cowboys. Some of their methods are brutal: they lasso them and then tie them to a tree, which strangles them until they fall to the ground; or they shoot a mare in the flank, which will attract her colt – the real target for this tried-and-tested manoeuvre. My companions approach the mare reluctantly. She has probably been shot down several days ago, judging from her swollen side and the smell of putrefaction. This terrible spectacle makes me ashamed to be a human.

Reaching the height of 1000 metres, we stop at Davies Plain Hut, where I stumble on an old wooden enclosure, sparing me the effort of unravelling and installing my own electric fence. I must keep Roxanne, River and Cooper safe from possible intruders. The landscape is forested with a blend of eucalypts. The Omeo gums', or *Eucaplyptus neglecta*'s, branches are as big as a baobabs' and covered with tough leaves. Interspersed among the forests are plains of snowgrass, and little streams of crystalline water, which I drink from next to my horses. This old log-hut is coiffed with a rusted corrugated-iron roof – a vestige of the past. It was built in 1909 to help the bushmen bringing their cattle to pasture. A large field, fringed with trees, surrounds it. I luxuriate in the peace of mind this spot provides, knowing my three horses will be safe in the enclosure. The hut is basic; I camp there inside the precarious-looking shelter. As I'm settling into my quarters, I meet the most extraordinary bird I've ever seen: a gang-gang cockatoo with grey feathers. His tufty, red-mohawked head gives him an insolent look. He seems to have made his home in this shelter. Towards dusk, the red-orange light fills the air with magic. I wander off with Fox and wash in an icy mountain stream, rushing over polished stones – a tough tonic …

Before leaving, the next day, I bandage the horses' fetlocks to protect them from sores caused by the boots. In trying to avoid one problem, another has been created. This difficult procedure adds a good half-hour to my morning preparations. The boots are hard to fit on and, with my hands covered with blisters and cuts, it's a tussle. Under the morning's great blue sky, we cross eucalyptus forests, before coming down to the Murray River plains that join the Alpine National Park. The Murray is 2530 kilometres long: its source lies in the Australian Alps, and it rambles through the land in many majestic meanderings before emptying itself into the Indian Ocean, south of Goolwa, near Adelaide. Oddly, its flow is weak because of groundwater-pumping, for the purposes of irrigation, and from being subjected to high levels of evaporation. The river dries up in periods of drought – and, as rain is scarce here, this happens often. Roads and elevated railways seem to hover over the grassy plains, but they are really crossing the Murray riverbed. Endemic species take shelter in the Murray's waters, like the big freshwater shrimp and the platypus. The river's banks are lined with red gums – which absorb a lot of the river water, too.

We tackle a path gullied by rains which have made large, round stones crop up at the surface and have dug enormous cavities. This path is dappled by the sunlight trying to break through the hotchpotch of large grey pines and eucalypts. As we reach a large plateau where we are to establish our camp, I spot a herd of brumbies in the distance. I've often heard about the Snowy Mountain brumbies, considered better specimens than those stigmatised as 'feral' because of their strong consanguinity and the arid or desolate areas in which they breed. I've been told that the Snowy Mountain brumbies are often seen in a more romantic light thanks to 'The Man from Snowy River'. Legend has it that the old stockman Jack Riley was the inspiration for Banjo Patterson's poem.

I settle my camp and install Roxanne, River and Cooper's enclosure. Then, I set off to meet the wild horses. I can see several beauties – dapple greys, and roans, their coats mixed through with white hairs. They appear to be in shining health. When I return to our camp at dusk, I catch sight of five or six of them coming towards us at a full gallop. Without thinking, I run towards them, yelling and waving my arms, and manage to get them to swerve away and flee. Another sleepless night to look forward to, listening out for my Roxanne, River and Cooper's bells …

Environmentalists are divided on the issue of brumbies – the proponents for preserving biodiversity condemn the damage they cause; the bushmen, on the other hand, are fervent advocates of wild horses as they are very useful to them.

The latter also assert the brumbies' cultural heritage value, wanting them to be named a protected species, considering that the early settlers would not have managed without them. Abandoned in favour of machines and returned to the wild, they proliferated. A hearty polemic opposes these two camps, in view of the large mountain territories that the Australian government took away from the breeders in order to transform them into national parks, under the banner of protecting local flora and fauna. But it's difficult and costly to manage such vast expanses, some of which are impenetrable, and they end up becoming overgrown with weeds and bush – fuel for bushfires.

I'm not alone in this camp site. It's an odd feeling: I feel I'm free-wheeling, skidding; to speak to humans again, to see human expressions, has me concentrating. It's not as easy as it seems. A couple in their fifties, hikers with a four-wheel drive, are already installed. I ask them to excuse the noise of my companions' bells. We get to talking, commenting on how beautiful the brumbies are. They tell me that, in their youth, they saw bushmen bringing their herds through this mountainous region. A bygone era …

On the way down, the vegetation becomes denser and more varied. The tall ferns reappear. On our last night in the state of Victoria, we reach another hut. Strung all along these wild territories, rooted in isolation, all these huts remind me of the ones in the European Alps. They're a lifesaver for riders, hikers, bush people and loners. Tonight, we're sleeping in the Dogman Hut – they all bear evocative names – then, I'm heading for the Murray. I've been looking forward to swimming from shore to shore in the longest river in Australia … Small pleasure, big reward.

In the morning, the manager of the Tom Groggin Station, a farm on 2000 hectares, established in 1860 and standing on the threshold of New South Wales, rides out to meet me. He's been warned of my passage and takes time to show me around the station's log cabins. You'd think you were in *Little House on the Prairie*. The green rolling hills with their blue-tinted mountains in the distance are so ubiquitous. Yet they always blow my mind away. The old cabin is preserved in its original condition, with its small paintings on the log walls, its nostalgic, old-fashioned objects: the presence of such witnesses to their vanished daily life, now claimed by history, have made these cabins a sought-after destination. Afterwards the manager escorts me to the frontier and points out the best place for us to cross the Murray. In this spot, the width of the river is a good 30 metres. We slide into the clean, cold water. My horses are immersed up to their necks and I lift my feet off the stirrups to avoid being drenched. Fox swims alongside, as is his wont; he loves the water. The man looks impressive astride his stock horse, the oldest breed in Australia, he tells me, imported from South Africa at the end of the seventeenth century. He shows us the way before leaving, wishing us the best of luck.

It's now the 12th of January and we've been on the Trail for nearly two months. Our arrival in New South Wales has cost us an enormous effort. We're leaving behind the most difficult section of the whole expedition. Treading a little path lined with ferns, we enter a dense forest, with streams running through it. I feel a real difference from the drier atmosphere of Victoria.

Slowly, stage by stage, not rushing it, we reach Kosciuszko National Park, the highest point in Australia. Entering this landscape, I am overwhelmed; its beauty rushes at me. The mountains so near the clouds, the river, the palette of greens, and the population of kangaroos with their wise, sad eyes, turn it into something that feels more imagined than seen. I've never seen nature exhibiting such splendour so completely. And I'm not the only one. Such unmitigated beauty attracts a crowd of people – hikers, fishermen, and families on an outing. It makes me realise how much Australians love their land, its beauty, its uniqueness.

I find us a peaceful spot on the shore of Geehi River, a mountain river, where my horses can feast. In their own way, they tell me how blissful it is to be here, rolling themselves in the grass they've been so happily consuming; the improved quality of this pasture is due to the cattlemen who used to bring their mobs here. Victoria and its steep summits have been extremely hard on the horses and they've lost weight, but they have proved their resilience. As for me, not being an athlete, all these vertiginous mountain paths, traversed on foot most of the time, have given me all sorts of aches and pains. I've got bruises everywhere, and my muscles are a chain of knots. I take my companions into the river to wash them. They love the freshness of the water and splash about in ecstasy. Then it's my turn, washing myself and my clothes in the pure water.

I meet two families, who, impressed by my odyssey, invite me to dinner. I'm keen to taste something different to my boring rations. In thanks, I take their kids bareback riding on Roxanne. These people are glamping rather than camping – the fresh dinner they produce is for me a godsend and a luxury. I eat like a horse, though probably not so daintily as my companions. We share a meal of meat, salads, fresh vegetables and good fun. I don't hold back when they offer me cold beer and wine. I love Australians' attitude – they're so warm, welcoming and friendly. Meanwhile, my hobbled horses continue grazing. These families appreciate my companions' calm temperament. Roxanne, Cooper and River have become used to camp life. Roxanne even comes begging near us during our dinner, which makes everyone laugh. At nightfall, when I'm preparing for bed, kangaroos also graze peacefully nearby. There's something Edenic about this harmony between humans and animals in the very heart of the wilderness.

At dawn, I'm woken by Roxanne, who's come to nibble the grass under my head, probably as a way to imply that it's time for us to move on. I linger a few minutes listening to the water and to a concert of birdsong before opening my tent. One bird attracts my attention: a black-and-white passerine, with a white beak and red eyes, and a song of pure melody. But the real artist is the flute-playing magpie; its unique and harmonious scales are so different from the cackling, cracking sounds that emanate from European magpies. The sun is peeping through the morning mist, which is borne up by the fresh air. Roxanne's, River's and Cooper's silhouettes give the scene an unerring peace. The promise of a beautiful day lies ahead.

This morning we're moving towards the small village of Khancoban, its inhabitants living at the foothills of the Snowy Mountains – a paradise for ornithologists. There, I intend to spend a few days rest to stock up on supplies and fill my companions' bellies. Friends of Finnie's also live around here and have invited me to sleep on their property, in a caravan near the water. I accept their proposal with alacrity.

When I leave Khancoban, it's confusing to realise that a choice of several tracks are open to me. These options are not mentioned in the Trail guide. The maps are about thirty years old and many things have changed, especially on the outskirts of small towns. Fishermen and hunters have created new paths with their four-wheel drives. I'm disheartened that I have to spend so much time searching for the right one. Now, I can't make up the lost time, and I end up only doing 10 kilometres before calling it a day, with a howl – as I do to signal when we've reached a camp near a welcoming brook.

The next day, we get through roughly 30 kilometres in about 8 hours. But when we've halted, and after unsaddling my horses, I realise that I forgot the electric tape for the enclosure and left it at the last camp. The few days' rest at Khancoban distracted me and relaxed my guard – my vital reflexes have been on the blink. I'm going to pay a high price for my forgetfulness. Even if it unravelled like Ariadne's thread, this enclosure was my safety net, my shield. Without it, I cannot continue my journey – and we're still in brumby country. My brain is whirring at three hundred miles an hour; I have to find a solution quickly. We've only got two more hours of daylight left and it's a seven-hour ride minimum to go back and then return from where we've come from. My only chance – the only solution I can come up with – would be to tie the two geldings to a tree with Fox and ride Roxanne, my rock, all the way back to retrieve the reel of electric tape. It'll obviously be faster with one horse. But this solution will be taxing and dangerous. River and Cooper hate being separated from the family we've formed and wouldn't fail to express their anxiety.

But I've got no choice. I decide to throw a tarp over my equipment and, my heart in my boots, I get myself ready to retrace my steps. I'm in an agony of uncertainty, when suddenly the coordinator for this section of the Trail, an older man I met at Khancoban, materialises on his dapple grey. He had transported his horse in his truck to a few kilometres away from my camp and decided to pay us an unexpected visit. When he learns what's happened, he proposes to retrieve the precious coil himself and return within two hours. I can't believe it. Finnie comes back to mind. My old mate, the bushman, was right – luck does exist.

We move towards a station called Jagumba, nestled in a deep valley of venerable trees along the Tooma River. Its owner, Barry Paton, welcomes me. This tall man, of about seventy-five years of age, proposes a stop in his home, and offers a bed and a shower. His wife is a vet. I look after my three companions and wash off the day's dust. Over a glass of rum-and-coke, which I accept with joy, just for once, Barry tells me about his love of brumbies, and relates stories from his youth when he'd catch brumbies and train them. He had even created a show called *The Man from Snowy River Spectacular*, in which he had these intelligent and agile horses perform all kinds of incredible stunts. He managed to teach one of them to leap on the back of a moving ute and another to climb on top of an enormous tyre lying flat on the ground and filled with earth – the horse would then turn around it. He even taught his old magnificent Appaloosa stallion to count. When he indicated the number three by raising three fingers, the horse scratched the ground three times with his hoof. He taught him to assume outlandish poses, like lying on the ground, bowing, sitting. This man, who used gentle training methods, has a gift. He shows me around his property with pride and with sadness because he has to put it up for sale. It's getting a bit too much for him, considering his age. His children are not interested in pursuing the same career path. The eternal story – each to their own life …

When we leave Jagumba Valley, we start climbing again to get across the Great Dividing Range from east to west. In the west, the landscape is wilder and more abrupt. We're reaching the highest point of the Trail at some 1700 metres. I can see the charred trees of past bushfires. The vegetation is changing drastically – the trees are becoming smaller and the grass isn't as lush for Roxanne, River and Cooper. Time is ticking by fast and I must be wary of the altitude. We follow the ridge of an imposing canyon, before crossing Tumut River – which is more of a torrent – on a wooden bridge. We then pop out into Happy Jacks Plain. A storm has pursued us all day and I feel really isolated in the bleak light of this austere, desolate environment. I hurry my friends along so that we can bivouac before the storm reaches us. Not finding any trees, I hastily create a makeshift enclosure using scrounged wood as stakes. A violent wind forces me to fasten everything securely. I try to put up my tent as fast as I can, and I store all the equipment inside it. A short distance away from us, the sky has turned pitch black. I've hardly driven in the last stake when rain starts lashing down on us. Water oozes inside the tent and I have trouble holding it up. Fighting against the gusts of wind, I fling my navigation gear and other fragile belongings into a waterproof bag and wait for the storm to abate. I can't make a fire and so, famished as I haven't swallowed a morsel since 4.30 this morning, I cook my dinner by lighting a gas cooker inside the tent – crazily dangerous, and to avoid at all costs, but needs must … I can see my horses, their backsides exposed to the wind, their heads down as a curtain of rain crashes onto them. I am so tired that I have hardly eaten my pasta before I fall asleep in wet clothes.

The next morning, happy to leave this place of woe, I pack all the gear in the pouring rain. A very soggy team, we head in the direction of a large artificial lake, Eucumbene Dam, a barrage, built in 1956, designed to supply the area with water. To find Providence, a town on the shores of the lake, two avenues are available – I choose the shortcut through the undergrowth. I use a compass to find my way through a labyrinth of dense and spindly trees. Luckily, my tough horses soldier on and don't complain. In the distance, I can see a large expanse of water; I can hear frogs, a multitude of birds, and have glimpses of kangaroos. We're still dripping wet, as is all my equipment. I wade and fight my way through a marshy terrain leading to a few fishermen's bungalows on the lake's shore. Convincing their owner to rent me one, in which to dry myself and spend the night, is no easy matter. Dripping, muddy, my appearance doesn't encourage him in the least.

For a few days now, River isn't working; he has had a swollen shoulder. He worries me. His morphology is different to that of the two others. The saddle doesn't sit as well on him. I call my friend Rachel in Canberra, three hours away. I met her when I was working in an Aboriginal community. She owns horses and understands the problems that can affect them. She drives over, finds us, and together we work out that the saddle has been applying points of pressure on River's back. Constrained by the absence of a vet in the area, we're forced to leave things as they are. Rachel has brought fresh supplies with her and spends the day with me.

On the edge of Kosciuszko National Park, again at 1500 metres, we're on a very narrow track, in a forest of snow gums. The pastel colours of the mountain landscape, the pale green leaves and fragile blue skies, all melt into a soft mist. We live in a watercolour, three days from Yaouk, the little town that heralds the end of Section 11. We still have a long way to go. At this altitude, the forecast is capricious and plays tricks on us, summer or not summer. Approaching Yaouk, we're descending onto a plain, when a sudden storm arises. Lightning strikes 20 metres from my horses, and they thrash around, flinching and sidestepping. Lightning pursues its course around us. Instead of keeping their usual pace, my companions change their gait; we're trotting, even galloping, in the last kilometres. My objective is an equestrian farm belonging to Peter Cochran, a well-known activist devoted to the brumby cause. He has set up a horse-trekking business in the mountains and offered me the use of his stables – an unmitigated joy after the storm. When he pays us a visit, he congratulates me on my mounts' good physical condition, but advises the use of penicillin for River; a series of injections is mandatory if I want to avoid an infection.

A relentless and ardent defender of the Snowy Mountain brumbies – in these mountains where one could accomplish nothing without them – the bushman and old parliamentarian underlines the 'deep link uniting the land, its inhabitants and the horses we protect. They're a symbol of freedom and are part of the cultural identity of this country.' He adds, 'We can't only call them a scourge – history and mythology are also important.'

According to the latest news, Peter Cochran seems to have been heard. In May 2018, the Australian government prepared a decree, the 'brumby bill', which confers on these mountain horses a heritage status.

To mention only Australia, what would the settlers in this gigantic land have accomplished without the help of horses? They were vital for so many things – for agriculture and cattle work, for the extraction and exploitation of gold and coal, for transport, for the management of forests, for construction work and for the post …

4

Canberra, Temporary Return to Civilisation

Section 10: Yaouk to the Jenolan Caves

613 kilometres

28 January to 29 February 2016

Sitting at the summit of a breathtaking chain of mountains, Yaouk is a locality of twenty-five inhabitants, 108 kilometres from Canberra. Rather than for its population density, it's been known, since 1820, as the historic crossroad for wool. Though on the one hand you will not often be bothered by the neighbours, on the other hand tourism is developing, attracting city dwellers on a quest for solitude. Fishermen dream of ensnaring the famous freshwater cod from Murrumbidgee River at the end of their line, and here they can do so in a paradise-like valley. We are met with this unique view on the 28th of January 2016, at the end of seventy-two days' walking and riding on the BNT, that immense trek of endless horizons, more than 5000 kilometres long, with its twists and turns, peak climbs and valley descents; the wild, the unpredictable, journey – in other words, *the Trail*.

Six hundred kilometres separate us from the Jenolan Caves, a vast system of grottos, cathedrals, and stalactites and stalagmites that I would have loved to visit; they could be compared to the Chasm of Padirac in the Dordogne. But as they're a tourist attraction, it wouldn't be safe for my horses; so I prefer to give it a miss.

This section of the Trail also crosses the capital territory of Canberra. Between Yaouk and Canberra, I enter the Namadgi National Park, where the still-uncertain weather has me stopping for the night in one of the old settlers' huts – preserved because of their heritage value. I'm not supposed to use it. I wonder if my horses' dung would disturb the hikers … but since I'm here, I stay. Built of stone and wood, with a corrugated-iron roof similar to all the others, and surrounded with pines and gum trees, its charm is deeply reminiscent of those in cherished books like Laura Ingalls Wilder's. I fall asleep on the floorboards in front of the fireplace. When morning comes, a light mist forms a halo around everything I look at. The serenity of the place gives me the feeling I could live here. For years I haven't had a home to call my own. I've been on a perpetual journey around the world and in remote places all around Australia, footloose since leaving school … but recently, each time I find myself in an attractive place with my horses, I imagine making my home there.

Around us, kangaroos are grazing, competing with my horses. For some reason, it bothers me. In my opinion, my horses need the precious grass to fill their bellies more than the kangaroos do. I'm like an unreasonable mother defending her offspring. There could be another reason for why their grass is vital to me. Being so in tune with my three friends I can't bear submitting them to a bridle and especially to a bit in their mouths anymore. I ride in a halter and communicate with them by the softest pressure, to which they immediately respond. In a way, we are more than a family; we are a common spirit with common needs and common goals. And I'm starting to sense that they too want to conquer this Trail. It has become our quest; not only mine.

Then, we leave our grassy haven and we're off on the Trail again; it's been raining all day. I'm drenched and soggy. Towards dusk, in the centre of a clearing, I stop at a new shelter, Horse Gully Hut. One of Peter Cochran's staff members meets me with a bale of hay. They had warned me there would be no feed for my horses – and they were right. I love these national parks strewn with refuges preserved 'in the raw'. As barely furnished as the others, this hut offers all one may need: an old iron camp bed (a luxury), chairs, log stools, a table, a shovel, a broom, a bucket for cleaning; not forgetting the essential component – the guest book, rich with stories. I love the rules, which expect that each traveller will leave the shelter clean and stocked up for the next visitor.

In front of the fireplace, I dry myself as close as I can to the fire; humidity is a relentless enemy. Graffiti has been carved in the wood by certain execrable guests, who seem to deem it essential to leave their mark everywhere they go. I spend the rest of the day listening to the rain machine-gun the roof – a sweet melody when one is safely sheltered. Through the window, I feed dates to my brumbies, who love them. I study my maps. I dine on soup in front of the fire. I fill my bottles with rainwater. I sing out loud and dance around in glee. I have myself a nice evening – one learns to entertain oneself.

By the time we go, the weather has become milder. Our track follows a stream – the Naas. We leave Namadgi Park and cross Carcoola, a private property whose manager offers me a roof reserved for the seasonal staff. The grass is excellent. I give my horses a day's rest to feast on it, and go and hunt wild boars with the family. The sport is not always well regarded in Australia, and is practised in a brutal way in general, using ferocious dogs with powerful jaws and sharp teeth, like pit bulls, bulldogs or Rhodesian ridgebacks. The dogs are kept in cages when they're not hunting, and are fitted with GPS collars, so their prey is left with little or no chance of survival. At the end of the hunt, the dogs themselves either return maimed or become lost and do not return at all. On their own in the wild, they breed, and attack cattle – they're not favourites with the farmers in the area.

But the people who've invited me to tag along on their hunt appear to be different. Brought up myself by a father who was a hunter and who respected nature, I accompanied him in France and in Spain after all kinds of various game. I've also followed the hounds on horseback. On my family's land, the animals that are shot are eaten and appreciated. My youngest sister, Diane, who lives in South Africa, worked for a while on animal reservations, taking tourists on horseback to see white rhinos, buffalos, zebras, giraffes and antelopes. Nature and wild animals have always been part of our lives. As such, I was curious about this Australian experience.

The two hunters prepare their dogs by donning them with protective harnesses and GPS collars. Once they're freed, highly excited, they know what's coming. The children are also part of the expedition. Dressed in camouflage gear, with daggers, knives and walkie-talkies, the hunters climb into their four-wheel drives and take me on a gutted stone track to where they think we'll meet some wild boars.

They're off. We must keep close to the sound of the mastiffs' barking. A young boy accompanies me. We run through thorny bushes on the hillside, a wild boar thunders a few metres past us, but the dogs are after another one. Out of breath, we catch up with them and see them assailing a small boar. They sink their teeth into the animal's throat and they don't let go. When one of the men comes up and ends it with his dagger, it's a flurry of excitement around us. The whole operation is quick; the animal doesn't have time to suffer too much. The hunter cuts him up and keeps the meat for the dogs, fearing it may carry too many diseases. Not culled sufficiently, the wild boars breed at a very fast rate. These pigs can be a scourge for crops, pastures, cattle and for breeders in general.

To thank the hunters for letting me tag along, I let their children ride bareback on Roxanne. Walking alongside, I hold her halter as she follows me gently. Horseriding teaches children to have good balance and to trust themselves. Also thanks to this hunting family, a neighbourhood farmer lets me sleep in his woolshed – the bush telegraph is an equivalent to the French 'Arabic telephone'. This farmer 'telegraph' turns out to be extremely helpful to me. The farmers warn each other of my arrivals and departures, and often provide a roof or some hay.

On the 31st of January, we're two days away from Canberra. I'm riding along a large asphalt road. With me astride one horse, flanked by the other two, I must make for a surreal and out-of-context picture, but drivers overtake us without slowing down. My maps prove useless. After the 2003 fires, when 500 houses were destroyed, buildings, like vertical concrete girders, deface the landscape, making the Trail maps obsolete. Thanks to Google Maps, I take a shortcut through the suburbs. Heads turn as we walk by. A garbage truck driver stops to look at us; people come out of their houses; drivers stare. My companions, thrown in at the deep end in the traffic, are so calm – I'm impressed. I congratulate myself on the training I put them through before our departure. They obviously remember it perfectly. I taught them to graze next to a road lined with electric tape, a metre from the carriageway, exposed to noise, trucks – to anything that roars with a motor: bombproof.

The Trail guide's directions are so archaic that a whole forest has been replaced by a mall. Google Maps is more precise and up to date. I decide to stick to the major arterial roads. I take a photo of the four of us, facing out in a row, stopped at a red light on one of those four-lane carriageways with a central median strip – a picture of two worlds colliding.

In the suburbs of the big city, we manage to locate the field reserved for the riders of the Trail. It's well indicated, with the appropriate signs, and, well fenced off, it offers beautiful green grass for the horses. Kathryn and Preston, the fellow riders I met on the Trail, are the last people to have made use of it, with their five horses two months ago. My friend Rachel meets us there. She lives in Yass, half an hour away from here. She offers to have me stay at her place – an offer that can't be refused. She also helps me to organise an appointment with a physiotherapist specialising in horses, so that their backs may be seen to.

Concerned with the good health of my dear companions, I ask a veterinarian for a general check-up of all three. River's shoulder, after a course of antibiotics, seems to have stabilised. The vet also determines, as my friend Rachel did, that the saddle doesn't fit his form perfectly, which creates inflammation. I adjust this using different saddle pads for him. As for the boots, they're not doing the job, and I buy new ones.

Once my horses are cared for, I get some supplies and am stunned to see my cousin Adrien le Gouvello turn up. He's on a business trip from Sydney. Single, good-hearted, with originality, and a good cook to boot … We're close in age and in temperament, and grant ourselves a crazy weekend. The highlight will be attending a rodeo in a small township nearby. Finnie will join us, as will Kathryn and Preston. I have Adrien discovering this completely different world; we even try a mechanical rodeo bull, but we French aren't really good at this kind of sport. One hand aloft and the other clasping the leather strap, we fall off in less than two seconds; seeing as the goal is to stay on for more than eight, this causes hilarity in the audience. Men crash to the ground, biting the dust, the audience applauds, the country music belts out, the announcer's bellow describing the exploits of those who can stay on beyond the pre-ordained eight seconds. Beer froths everywhere, people dance on tables. Meanwhile, the rodeo – the real one – lasts well into the night.

The next day, in spite of my hangover, I manage to find a saddler who can modify my pack saddle. I enjoy working with leather and do a few of my own repairs on my remaining equipment. I stay for hours in the workshop – I love this dying craft.

Warned that I cannot go through the capital with my

companions, I decide to take advantage of this to promote my cause, as well as the Guy Fawkes Heritage Horse Association's and its program. Rachel and I imagine organising a kind of parade up the boulevard leading to Parliament. At the last minute, lacking time and means, I round up a few people who have followed my adventures on social media. Two young women, Tania and Lara, join us. One rides Cooper and the other has her own horse. With my brumbies, parading down the three-lane carriageway road without a flinch, we reach the very contemporary Parliament building, surrounded by a manicured lawn that one feels like rolling on.

If you are approaching the building from atop a horse, with the firm intention of taking photographs and videos, obdurate policemen will stop you in your tracks and advise you to decamp. Sure enough, they try to make us back off. I laugh, explaining that my horse is wild, that he bites and kicks. I advise him not to try to come any closer. The policeman, a tad overwhelmed, goes off to find his superior. His chief turns up and asks us, 'Are these the Guy Fawkes National Park brumbies?' First question, first surprise. Because he has one himself and obviously supports our cause. This is an improbable stroke of luck. He lets us take pictures and videos on the Parliament lawn. I unfold my tarp, on which I have tacked a sign saying, 'Wild at heart, riding BNT with Guy

Fawkes Heritage Horses'. It can't be said we didn't snatch up the opportunity of exhibiting ourselves in front of Parliament, or that we were routed out.

After my whirl in Canberra, we walk through a succession of villages bearing the names Hall, Gundaroo, Taralga, where the hiking tracks become softer, easier. These country townships have character, and still possess their old buildings. Apart from the lovely grass and water, the main attraction is the pubs. There, drinking a good beer, I get information from the locals, the old-timers of the bush. Most of the bivouacs are the Travelling Stock Reserves (TSR), the paddocks reserved for cattle. They're usually situated near rodeo camps, because the drovers move their herds back and forth between their winter pastures and their summer ones. The possible stops on the way are organised with rodeo grounds.

Upon leaving Hall, I'm told that the river is dry. I must find an alternative for this lack of water for the 37 kilometres of road running between Hall and Gundaroo, where I plan to pay a visit to Kathryn and Preston. But this morning, I've been asked to do a live phone-interview on ABC at a very precise time. The clock is ticking, and I can find no favourable place for us to stop with horses on this windy part of the Trail; occasional traffic can make it dangerous. That's when I catch sight of an entrance to a private property along the asphalt road. Pressed for time, I tie my horses to a white fence, with the feeling I shouldn't be doing this.

I move away for a few minutes to do the interview. When I return to my companions, I open Cooper's saddlebag, and a can crashes to the ground. This frightens Cooper and he tugs at his halter. His fear infects the other two, who now rip away from the fence, which turns out to be plastic. They smash it down and gallop away onto the road in the middle of the cars, dragging pieces of plastic paling behind them. The sight is terrifying. My blood runs cold at the thought of causing an accident, one of my biggest fears from the start. I manage to catch hold of Roxanne and calm her, but Cooper and River are still at a full gallop, panicked by the debris trailing in their wake. Fox and I are left staring. Before all is lost, I try yelling out my rallying call at the top of my lungs. At this, they stop and calm themselves. I've instilled the meaning of this call into them since they were adopted: at every feeding time I call to them, so they come to me before I hand over their food. On the road, the traffic has frozen. Patiently, the drivers wait till I've caught up with the two fugitives. A big scare – the consequences could have been a hundred times worse.

River has a small wound on his hind leg, from where a piece of fence has struck him; Cooper is all right. I'm shaking from head to toe, and wondering how I can compensate the property owner for their fence. Nothing like this has happened before now. A bandage and a disinfectant will sort out River's cut. I phone Preston, who lives close by, in Gundaroo, and we decide to go to the village – the horses need to be sorted out first. I then return to find the owner of the fence. I express how sorry I am and we agree on a compensation; he appreciates my honesty. When I leave him, it's still very hot on the road and we're going to a place without water. The driver of a maintenance water truck, equipped with a cistern, stops and waves at me. He offers some water to the horses – neither of us has a bucket, so they drink from my hat.

At Gundaroo, the police station, with its white picket fence, looks like a wood and corrugated-iron doll's house. The path to the door is lined with pink rose bushes. It's the 15th of February; we've been on the Trail for ninety-one days. The sun is beating down on us, and to save Fox's legs for a few kilometres I pick him up and settle him on my horse's saddle, walking by his side. He hates this position and makes no effort to find his balance. He got hit on the head by a horse's hoof when he was six months old – his memory of it is keen, and he has no sympathy for the Equidae. He bears a grudge against them and heartily despises them, especially as I give them so much of my attention; Fox doesn't appreciate sharing my affection. Roxanne, River and Cooper, however, are more tolerant.

When I reach the TSR paddock, I'm distraught to discover Cooper's first wound in the three months we've been travelling, because of friction from the pack saddle. It's broken the skin slightly. I don't see any remedy apart from time; any ointment would weaken the flesh around the wound even more. It's the worst of injuries, because it has to heal of its own accord. Luckily, thanks to my rotation system, River is more available to me, which will help Cooper to rest and recoup for a few days. I don't intend for my companions to pay the price of finishing the Trail at any cost.

We go past Crookwell, a small town at 900 metres in altitude. Its two thousand inhabitants have converted from growing cereals to being 'spud diggers', as they call themselves. I sleep at a rodeo camp, after drinking beers and chatting to the locals, which is now a well-established habit. In these places, everybody speaks to everybody. It's rare to stay alone at the bar.

Towards Taralga, the asphalt road lies under a beating sun. Halfway there, we encounter a sign on the side of the road that says 'Aliénor and brumbies,' with a can of water and bucket for the horses. There's also an apple, a muesli bar and a bottle of water for me. This anonymous gesture tugs at my heart. After Victoria, where the water is always pure and tastes good, it's a shock to need a special bottle with a water-straw filter – but, in New South Wales, you need one to drink directly from a river or a dam.

On the road lies a rotting, dead wombat. Once in Taralga, the rodeo-ground keeper forbids me to let my horses graze peacefully; he demands that they stay in the stables. I find some hay and sleep with them in the stall. After being stationary all night, they wake with swollen legs, and this is compounded by their 40 kilometres on asphalt the day before.

When I leave Taralga, a proactive and resourceful environmental activist, with an apt and predestined name, Mark Forest, comes to meet me. I had gotten to chatting with this defender of endangered species in the Crookwell pub. With his activist slogan 'Respect Existence or Expect Resistance', he has fallen into the habit – disguised as the animal he's campaigning to protect – of handcuffing himself to deforestation trucks. He possesses a whole gamut of animal costumes, from the koala to the wombat to the kangaroo. Of course, he's sympathetic to my brumbies' cause, and he hands me a kangaroo suit, which I slip on while I'm still astride Cooper, before posing for a series of photographs. The fifty-year-old journalist has bought land in the area that he wants to transform into a wildlife sanctuary.

From there, we stumble upon a house which is lost in the middle of nowhere. I ask the owner if she can give us some water. She makes her barn, which has a water cistern next to it, available to us and invites us to dinner with her family. Those who live in the bush have the reputation of being kind, open and caring; it's not usurped here. When I leave at dawn, my hostess is up so we can spend a day's ride together. We'll follow the Blue Mountains by crossing a pine forest. I'm disappointed not to be able to enter into this mountain chain – the Trail follows it but without venturing into it. I learn that the mountains reach up to 1100 metres and that they're part of the Great Dividing Range, which runs up the Australian coast for 3000 kilometres. Its spectacular gorges were carved out by rivers, but its blue haze has been bestowed upon it by its forests.

I had made contact with Martin and Hazel, the coordinators of this Trail section, and they insisted on inviting me to their property. Of all those with whom I've dealt, they're the most generous. They don't hesitate in having us over for a few days, and, thanks to them, Cooper's wound can begin to heal.

The first national park in the world, Yellowstone – created in the United States in 1872 by Judge Cornelius Hedges, the senator of Montana – runs across Wyoming, Montana and Idaho. It preserves this part of the Rocky Mountains in its pure and natural state. Following the Americans' footsteps, the colonial government of New South Wales declared a terrain of 15,090 hectares near Sydney as a royal national park. At its origin, it was more of a leisure park, easy and convenient for city dwellers. Judging the country's natural state as hostile, the new Royal Zoological Society of New South Wales introduced vegetal and animal species. From then on, each state of the Federation brought its own response to these two different approaches to national parks.

Today, Australia has more than five hundred national parks, some of which are World Heritage listed. In the past 150 years, the depletion of natural resources, the extinction of native species combined with the proliferation of invasive ones, the growing influence of environmentalists, the heavy use of small streams for agriculture, global warming – all these have led to an increased awareness of nature's precarious position. Some of the damage is, however, irreversible. The idea that humans are not the owners of this beautiful planet but part of a system of global interdependency with all other forms of life is starting to be accepted. The upkeep of these parks is costly, and the high number of brumbies is only one aspect of this expenditure: how to limit the proliferation of these animals without enacting shocking massacres, and in which park, without forgetting the eternal question – at what cost? Canberra is debating on this subject, I am told, to find a solution to this issue.

Australia's voice is never silent ... As if the country itself were relating its woes and victories, I can't help thinking of all this as I finish Section 10 of the Trail, drawing closer and closer to the north, towards the tropical heat expected at the end of our trek. Our little team has not been idle ...

5

Dingo Howls

Section 9: The Jenolan Caves to Aberdeen

320 kilometres

29 February to 20 March 2016

My father's, Anne-Henri's, birthday is the 29th of February.
He was born in a leap year – that's how the chips fell. Even
in the middle of nowhere, I think of him with tenderness. He
doesn't understand this venture of mine, and especially not
the way I've led my life until now. Coming from a traditional
family of eleven children, he didn't *appreciate* – and that's
an understatement – my leaving school right before the
baccalauréat, France's secondary certificate of education. In
my parents' eyes, studies are important, particularly if one
wants women to be equal to men. I'm the most rebellious of
his four daughters. Insubordinate from a very early age, I was

bored and felt hemmed-in at school. My father was a rebel, too, in his time – my grandfather, Gouvello L'Africain, offered more chastisements than support on his return from overseas. Anne-Henri should remember it!

I'm ruminating on this when we reach our next camp at nightfall. The roof of a collapsed hut provides us shelter among its ruins, where I can keep out of the rain. I make a feast of porridge and wild blackberries for breakfast, picking a supply of berries for later. Cooper's back can finish healing, thanks to these extra days of rest.

Next on the programme for our trek is a new string of country villages. I stop at Hampton, to find the usual pub and chat with the locals. Little by little, I am getting the feeling that this expedition is becoming a pub crawl. Not that this is a problem for me; I love a cool beer. In the pub, I meet authentic characters – it's the social aspect of my journey. I'm open to it, and I like talking to the regulars. The information they give me about the terrain, and their warnings, are my landmarks, my dictionary and my weather forecast. They're generous with information deriving from their rich experiences, and this saves me a lot of time and hardship.

In this way, I get to chatting with Dave, a bald man in his fifties, full of smiles, and with a pronounced beer belly, a very strong Australian accent and a staccato beer intake.

He invites me over to his place with my horses. He lives in Rydal, but I'm always wary when someone tells me that they live 'close by'. If it's on my way, that's okay; but if it's beyond a certain number of kilometres, then it's a no-go. We leave the pub in an advanced state of inebriation; I have difficulties finding my companions that night. I can't see the field for the horses ...

The next day, I've got such a hangover, it's hard to get going ... and then rain comes to the party. Towards ten o'clock – I must have been riding for two or three hours; I'm not quite sure – Dave comes by in a pick-up to see how we're going. Of course, he offers me a fresh beer from his esky. *'A "hair of the dog" will set you right.'* I think to myself, *A beer at 10am? What the hell, why not?!* With his jolly face and debonair demeanour, he kindly offers to host us. I check that he doesn't live further than 2 kilometres from the next section of the Trail, and accept his invitation. I put the pack saddle in his vehicle so I can ride faster. We set off to Rydal, a small country village with a proud heritage, and flowerbeds of thousands of jonquils, which visitors come to admire in September. I leave my stuff at the rodeo ground – where you won't see a blade of grass however long you look. My host reveals himself to be a true bushman, a farm manager, an ardent collector of old stuff – of everything and anything that has been lying around: coils of rope, old tools, old cars, bits of string, all that is obsolete and forgotten ... With his neighbours, Laura and Will, we spend two days laughing and drinking. The Trail gives you moments of relaxation and whimsy, and I take them when they come. Dave also takes me waterskiing on a nearby lake with his grandchildren. For a solitary nomad, this is a merry change from the dusty trek.

But it's time to say goodbye ... I ride past Wallerawang, where Charles Darwin stayed in 1836. He describes the surrounding wildlife, such as the mysterious platypus, in *The Voyage of the Beagle*. The Great Western Railway crosses the town, a link with civilisation in this immensity of mountains, forests and plains. As we leave Wallerawang, on a narrow path lined with gigantic lacy ferns, we're submerged into a dense, dark forest. A world of green. We climb up a canyon with a spectacular view over thousands of hectares of giant eucalypts stretching to the horizon and we discover Wolgan Gap, a canyon that has dug itself out of a rockface of enormous grey-and-ochre sandstones. The butterflies are becoming bolder around me. Dave had explained: 'When a butterfly alights on you, you'll know that you're at one with nature.'

These rocks are very high and imposing. They form steep cliffs with landslides of boulders, dotted with compact shrubs filtering sunlight. The terrain is hard on the horses' feet; I've fallen into the habit of setting River loose behind us. He follows his own rhythm, and always catches up. If he stops for too long and loses sight of us, he'll gallop himself into a lather to find us. But the passages are so steep that I have to dismount and take each horse down, one after the other, picking out a path with hairpin bends, so as not to fall. The agility of my brumbies impresses me, including the one who's carrying the pack saddle. I must on no account walk in front of them, but at their side, in turn, to avoid the possibility of them falling onto me. We're in the gardens of Stone National Park – its eponymous name echoes the magic of its landscape. After imbibing generously from the three last watering holes, being alone in the bush again, in an alcohol-free zone, feels like a sanctuary.

With a heavy heart, though, I've had to leave Fox behind again, this time with Laura and Will, Dave's neighbours. In Wollemi National Park, I'll ride by ranger stations, and I don't want to cause issues with the Trail regulations, which prohibit dogs. I climb Baal Bone Gap again, to cross a mountain pass. The view is a jewel beyond price, but it's also the paradise of four-wheel drivers, all engines roaring. Once on top of these rocks, my faithful friends, their manes blowing in the wind, don't have a blade of grass to eat; Laura and Will bring me a highly appreciated bale of hay. Going from a fern-covered place to a park of gigantic trees without an atom of edible vegetation is disconcerting.

That night, on the windy pass, surrounded by moaning trees, I lie down without Fox, bunkered up in an eerie atmosphere. Towards one in the morning, I'm awoken by Cooper's worried snorts warning me that something odd is afoot. I hear masculine voices – after all, I'm in a forest which is accessible to everyone. I part my tent's flap slightly and see a torch flashing on my brumbies. I sense the male voices are drunken. I've lost my SPOT tracker and have asked Dave to try to find it for me. So, without Fox, I feel even more vulnerable.

At this precise moment, I sense panic taking hold of me. If I step out of my tent, I'll reveal that I'm a woman, alone. In this kind of situation, I freeze. For the moment, they haven't seen my tent. I stay hunched up, armed with my one knife – a ludicrous protection. My father had insisted that I carry a rifle with me, but I'd refused, thinking I'd never want to get to the moment I'd have to point it at someone. And Australian laws are very strict on weapons, which are meant to be kept in a safe.

The three men – I've ascertained they are three – are drunk and boisterous. They continue bothering my horses. Left with just enough mobile network to make a call, I punch in the number of a policeman I met in the pub who gave me his details in case of danger – without a doubt, these pubs have multiple virtues. Keeping my voice as low as I can, I tell him what's going on. He says he'll warn his mates at the local police station. He advises me to hide myself behind Roxanne if things turn ugly. Time passes, an hour feels like a century. I can still hear them hollering. My horses are exhibiting signs of real unrest and I can't go out and reassure them. Finally, the men leave in their four-wheel drive. Half an hour later, two policemen turn up, stunned to see my tent in the middle of nowhere. They reassure me and go to patrol the forest in search of the drunks, but I find it impossible to get back to sleep. I come to the realisation that if Fox *had* been with me, his barking would have alerted them to my presence. Strange coincidence – his absence this time may have saved me from possible dire straits. I've got a passionate bond with my dog, my brother in humanity. I've been taking him everywhere for ten years – except when national park rules separate us.

At daybreak, we descend the pass on a rocky path. In spite of the boots on their front hooves, my companions show signs of being footsore. Every morning, I continue putting bandages on them. I also give them stretching exercises and massages just like the professional physiotherapist in Canberra – a specialist in endurance races – taught me to. In a landscape steeped in a blue haze, Wollemi National Park's vertiginous peaks offer us a view out of this world – a palette of red ochre and intense green overlooking the sandy rivers at their feet. Then the Trail sees us through Capertee Valley, in a 135-kilometre pass, lost and sublime, crossing the Blue Mountains, which the pioneers took forty years to get through. For a time, men extracted rock oil from the shale.

After a spectacular descent, we thread our way along a passage through the rock, and pop out in a valley. The terrain softens. I see an enormous lizard climbing a pine tree: a goanna monitor. A metre long, he hangs onto the bark with his claws. He looks at me and I acknowledge him. Goannas are everywhere, I realise, sunbathing on tree trunks, warming up their black-and-yellow striped skin. In the past, Aboriginal teenagers taught me to hunt and eat them. They'd walk in the desert to find the cavities in the sand – a sign of the goannas' habitat. If you see tracks on the threshold of a large hole, you know it's in there. You have to dig with a kind of crowbar until you reach a goanna's tail. Then you have to pull it out and kill it by smashing its head in one fell swoop with a stone or a tree trunk. If the lizard manages to escape, the children run after it, hollering and throwing stones at it when it manages to take refuge up a tree. From an early age, many Aboriginal children learn valuable hunting skills. The flesh of the goanna tastes like chicken, and is cooked on a wood fire and shared. The goannas I see today are much too big, though – good for them. Anyway, I'm not in hunting mode.

In this valley of plains and pastures, dominated by rocky-faced mountains on all sides, we arrive at Glen Davis, an old oil-extraction site, where I see the ruins of the refinery – a witness to an industrial past. This place is now a land of pastures and cattle-raising. A piece of blue sky, streaked with pink clouds and shafts of light, puts the mountains on stage, as though in a Turner painting. On the horizon, I can see a few showers carving out dark panels of grey with slashes of bright white sunlight. If I could hear music at this minute, it would be all of Vivaldi's *The Four Seasons* happening all at once, illuminating my day.

When we reach Glen Alice, a bit of a ghost town, with its old church and its community hall, I've got my eye on the small cemetery; full of tasty grass, it's the perfect enclosure for my three horses. Surely a little horse manure can't hurt, but in fear of offending someone I settle for the community hall grounds. Dave joins me with his grandchildren. He's found my SPOT tracker and has come to say goodbye. Afterwards, I meet a bushman who asks me to train his horses, which is impossible – I'd lose too much time and never be able to finish this. In this place where only a few farmers still hang on, he's the first human being I meet, apart from Dave of course.

We're back climbing mountains and scrambling up steep cliffs, when suddenly gusts of wind and rain swoop on us. I have been joined by Gisela, Carlston, and Laura, an English photographer. a Sydney-based production company, they came in a four-wheel drive to meet me and to document some of my expedition. Sopping wet, I hurry to find shelter from the storm. A wood and corrugated-iron lean-to on top of the mountain fits the bill, and I cover up my equipment. The sky's so black it feels like night. I unravel the electric tape to surround my brumbies and wait for the end of the downpour. The four-wheel drive hasn't managed to climb up here ... Just on the day a filming crew turns up for a shoot, an unreliable weather forecast comes to the party. Under the shelter, I sit on my lambskin and fall asleep looking at shooting stars.

Sitting under the lean-to on the promontory, at the top of the canyon, I see daylight breaking through the trees, unveiling a view of such majesty that I scramble up. Jumping up and down on the sandstone rocks covered with yellow and blue-green lichen, I lift my arms and cry out, '*Aouh! Aouh!*

Aouh!' – the dingo howl, the dingo cough – as if Fox were here with me in spirit, as if the freedom of Australia were in my gut. Soon I'm howling like a maniac – a stranger in this land where I feel mysteriously at home. My horses and I have reached the top of the world. My cries echo as if nature itself were answering. The sun, as yet barely a trace of golden embers, draws its shimmering line across the phenomenal view. The dusty green of the trees touches the blue and violet at the heart of the canyon. And I howl and howl …

I haven't been keen to involve media in my expedition as the constraints this would create could slow me down. By the same token, it's a way to publicise the cause I'm trying to defend. When the film crew leaves us, I feel free at not being bothered by their requirements anymore, even though Gisela and Carlston are genuine and kind people, and have believed in me and supported our cause from the start.

We continue following the sandstone ridge – which morphs into an imaginary village every time I blink. Then we descend into the canyon on a steep path with, on our left, a cliff-like face with different strata going from beige, to pink, to orangey hues. Vegetation returns, luxuriant. The weather comes back, too: blue skies, splashes of light reflecting on the polished sandstone of the rock face. The earth is red. Gigantic ferns undulate, and trees, running through a riot of greens, drip away the night's rain. We're alone with the birds' chorus, under the spell of the landscape. In the afternoon, my companions and I are climbing up again when yet another storm announces itself. We're progressing towards Nullo Mountain, a high plateau in the middle of the peaks, and one more breathtaking view over Wollemi National Park, with its wild vegetation and abrupt shifts in altitude – Australian landscape at its most rough, wide and open.

The bluish haze of dawn shrouds the mountains. A grey bellbird's cry pierces the air around me and makes me jump. I answer him. Soon a whipbird also answers back in a contrapuntal with his mate. I join in the conversation, I join in the rhythm of the bush, feeling like a regular Saint Francis of Assisi. Perhaps it's because this place was a sea floor millions of years ago that the landscape surrounding us rises and falls like waves on the horizon, interrupted by rocky spurs as tall as cathedrals in the mist.

My companions, whom I have stopped in order to concentrate on the bird calls, so new to my ear, and this unearthly view, are patiently waiting. Week after week, month after month, with Roxanne, Cooper and River, we've managed to form a family. Our trust is mutual. Our instinctive understanding of each other helps us face the challenges and the pitfalls we've thus far encountered on the Trail. We have a code and a ritual. I speak to them constantly during the day. I gently caress around their eyes to rid them of flies. I show them my affection and gratitude. Yes, a horse smiles, licks, kisses, sniffs. 'He obeyed me as if I were his own brain, not his master,' says Emperor Hadrian of his horse Borysthenes in Marguerite Yourcenar's *Memoirs of Hadrian*.

I'm exacting with them, but only because the Trail is. They're three, I'm alone. I can't let them overstep the mark or walk all over me – this is difficult enough as it is. I never hit them, or use any form of violence towards them, but they have to respect the rules. Of the three, Roxanne, the only female, is the one who tests them. Once or twice she left us, and I didn't try to pursue her: I know she doesn't want to be separated from her two mates. Sometimes at night, River and Roxanne like to come close to the fire to heat their bellies. When they graze, they never move away from each other. If they do, I follow like a shepherd keeping an eye on her flock. I walk alongside them with a bird guide, a bit of water, peanuts. I organise my time so that they can eat freely what they enjoy. Once satiated, when grass is abundant, they come and rest next to me. A feeling of belonging connects us. When my tent or my equipment are inside their enclosure, they never shove or overturn anything. I'm only wary of Roxanne, the greedy one – she'll nose about to find food. When I hobble them to let them graze at will before I've set up the enclosure, I only have to sound off my rallying cry for them to return to camp of their own accord. Then I'll always give them a reward, like copra, muesli or some other treat.

In the morning, religiously, I brush my long hair, which would become a wild nest if I didn't take care of it. I braid it, get dressed, then pack up my 'bed'. I must never look like a slob on a jaunt. My horses have grace; I must have, too. Then, I light up my gas stove to boil water for my coffee and prepare the porridge with muesli. Still puffy-eyed, I swallow my breakfast in the dark. Sometimes, I put on some good music to motivate myself and give me a bit of zest – often 'Roxanne' by *The Police,* which I sing at the top of my lungs.

Then, I store my camp away and take care of my horses. In this order, every day, it's a discipline. I prepare them, following a long procedure. I give them all the care they need. I brush them, I clean their hooves, filing them, too, if necessary. I also give them a back massage, which they adore, and I look after all their small aches and pains. I inspect them scrupulously. I take note of everything. I've taught them to line up in front of me like in a parade. I talk to them as if I had a row of privates reporting to me. My equipment neatly placed at my feet, they know every inflexion of my voice and that they mustn't budge. When I'm astride them during the day, they all understand that I sometimes dig out something nice to nibble from my saddlebags. They turn around, expecting me to share, which I don't fail to do. Seen from the outside, our outfit isn't much to write home about. Yet, I'm so grateful to my horses, without whom this journey would have been impossible on so many levels. With them, in total harmony with nature, we have slowly, but freely, ambled through this wild, wild world.

We're passing through Widden Valley, which offers splendid views of strangely shaped peaks. One of them is called the 'Cat's Ears'. Clouds of butterflies fill the air. We're crossing a wide plain of swaying waves of high grasses. A few windmills lighten the landscape on which well-fed, well-looked-after cattle graze peacefully. Cooper lags behind to snap up a few mouthfuls of grass on the way, and we end up arriving at Widden Stud, owned by a well-known thoroughbred breeder. These racehorses were created in the eighteenth century with English mares and Arabian stallions. This stud is one of the most prestigious in Australia: world famous, established in 1866, it has stayed in the same family for 150 years. It has produced the champions that have won 10 per cent of the best races in the country – an impressive result. Surprisingly, the stud has all this time remained a farm, with a bit of cattle, too. The property is sparkling, squeaky-clean, with attention and care towards every detail. It houses impeccably kept old buildings and, what attracts me most of all, vast enclosed pastures, which my brumbies will relish – without, of course, mingling with the other horses. No misalliances! Warned of our arrival, the owner, in his forties and in perfect shape, courteously invites me to visit his domain, and authorises me to put my equipment in a small hut, where I will be able to sleep. A sign announces 'Hilton' rather ironically, considering the state of the place. The abode is so dusty, brimming with rat and mice droppings, that I decide to camp outside. Three days' rest are welcome to my horses, who happily play and graze hobble-free in this idyllic location. My young geldings have trouble leaving these lush blue-green pastures sown with fresh lucerne. They gorge themselves and appreciate the visits by beautiful mares on the other side of the fence who come to meet them – a respite in our nomadic lives.

Following Widden Brook, we leave this wide valley. Cut by a dam, it gives birth to a lake, reflecting the sky in its mirror surface. We start climbing a mountain path again, on our way to Sandy Hollow, which seems to come straight out of a Western; nothing is missing, not even the train station or the coal-fired steam engine. I'm happy – I've got an appointment to meet Laura and Will, who are bringing Fox back to me. There are no more national parks on our way, for the time being.

While we were apart, Fox got into a fight with a large hunting dog and is in bad shape. He has a wound on his thigh and a bite on his ear. We move on again, but 10 kilometres from our next planned camp, on a cattle reserve, I notice he's having trouble walking. His wound is bleeding again, so I carry him in my arms. Eighteen kilograms is quite heavy to carry, especially on foot, and my arms are crying for mercy. When a car comes by and stops, I ask the driver if he can drop him at our next bivouac on the travelling stock reserve. When I get there, Fox greets me like the Messiah. I call Erica, who knows someone working in a neighbouring stud. She kindly comes to get him, to take him to a vet near Aberdeen. The verdict is heavy: two weeks of medical care and attention are necessary. Erica's friend needs to keep him during that whole time for him to be Trail-fit again. I'm devastated to lose him once more.

On that day, I'm surprised to receive a visit from Belinda Ritchie, the only woman to have finished the BNT completely, with three horses, like me. She offers to provide support until the next stage – this goes straight to my heart. She tells me she has a large debt to pay, for the many people who helped her during her trek; supporting those attempting the same adventure is a way of settling it. We arrive in Aberdeen, a cute, sleepy little town – the last one in this marvellous section – and we go and have a toast at the pub. I'm camping on the rodeo ground. The manager offers me a shower, and the local Catholic school, St Joseph's High School, puts a lovely paddock at my disposal – I know three friends of mine who'll appreciate this. Then, I see Fox for three too-short days during my rest.

On the 21st of March, our outfit reaches Hunter Valley, a region rich in studs, vineyards and mining industries.

6

So Far, So Good!

Section 8: Aberdeen to Ebor

417 kilometres

27 March to 24 April 2016

We're heading towards one of the loveliest sections of the Trail, the Oxley Wild Rivers National Park, full of endless rain forests and sumptuous gorges – yet another Australian World Heritage site. We're 560 kilometres from Sydney, inching ever closer to tropical temperatures. Upon leaving Aberdeen, the asphalt road is covered with millions of flies. The land is starting to dry up severely. The road I'm on runs through another region of prestigious studs. I pay a visit to Erica's friend, who took Fox to the vet. She works in a stud that is drawn with military precision. Ease and functionality define its solid fences and training ground – home to Australia's most well-known racing mare, Black Caviar.

A change of scenery: later in the evening, I find myself in a lost township. We're staying in the field behind the church, happy to dispose of and enjoy a modicum of grass – we could have encountered worse. The moon is high, and an echidna is coming out of the high grass!

Two days out from arriving in Barrington Tops National Park, one of the country's jewels, I'm disappointed to learn that we can't ride through it. A private landowner refuses passage to riders across his land. Anglo-Saxon law is different from French and English law, which respect rights of way. We're forced to take a longer route, through Nundle village, which has 289 inhabitants, and log cabins.

Today, 27th of March, is my birthday. We've been on the Trail for 132 days, travelling for four months and ten days. I'm still a day's ride from Nundle, where my friends Kathryn and Preston – who've come to the neighbourhood to collect a horse – grab the opportunity to have a drink, or even two, with me. Located at the foot of the Great Dividing Range, this small township lived through the goldrush of 1852. Since then, at the end of March each year, the Nundle Go for Gold Chinese Easter Festival is held, attracting more than fifteen thousand visitors. It's a festive atmosphere and the colourful crowd is drawn from everywhere, fascinated by the legend of the gold-diggers. I set up camp behind the pub, so I'm ready to go … The pub owner has accepted having my brumbies in his fields. My friend and saddler John Burton takes the opportunity to ride over on his motorbike for a visit, and makes repairs to my saddle. At this stop, I also receive all sorts of supplies that I had sent ahead for the weeks to come … Provisions follow the troupes.

After Nundle, still on our detour, we travel through a pine forest, taking a dirt road, which is dangerous for us. Gigantic logging trucks roar past, without a sideways glance for my trio, stirring up a blinding and asphyxiating cloud of dust as they overtake us. Always on the alert, ready to react when I can hear one coming, I swerve away.

We reach a cattle reserve, and I meet a woman I've heard about, who's following the Trail on foot. Her eleven-year-old daughter is behind her on a thoroughbred horse, accompanied by two little pack donkeys. They left from Healesville before me, but, progressing faster, I've now caught up with them. We had a lot of telephone conversations before we finally met. I'm impressed by her daughter, Zaydee, who's managing the expedition very well. The duo sometimes relies on the support of a friend with a four-wheel drive, who brings them supplies. The young girl doesn't have a bell around her horse's neck, and I offer her one in memory of the day Kathryn and Preston gave me my first bell. We separate our animals. Her thoroughbred chestnut proves himself to be very attached to the two little donkeys – they form a close-knit team. Because of the lack of grass and our very different mounts, we decide not to share the road. Riding alone has its charm.

That night, I feel like enjoying the night sky without my tent. Rather than a five-star hotel, I have all those above. I drive two stakes into the ground, on which I tie a tarp. Then, in front of the fire and under my canopy, lit up by sparks and flame, I drink to the heavens. Unfathomable happiness. I fall asleep near the glowing embers, but upon waking, after having communed with the Milky Way previously, the harsh realities of raw nature bring me back to earth with a thump. Under a solid drizzle that drenches without slaking our thirst, I look for water in this eucalypt and pine forest, with its undergrowth of ferns, and ask the logging truck drivers where I could find a spring. I'm told of a stream nearby, but warned about the leeches. They're right: I discover a perfect clearing with luscious grass for my horses. But the feast comes at a price. I get out of there covered in leeches, and my brumbies' legs are bleeding. I spurn their medicinal virtues and spend a long time pulling off these parasites, creating small wounds, even if their bites do not seem to bother the horses. I remove the ones on my person afterwards – they are stuck to my ankles and my wrists – with a knife tip; burning them is also a good method. The leech episode is stored away in my mind along with the other inconveniences of life amid unspoilt nature.

On one particular bivouac, a fairytale awakening near a swamp awaits us. Cloudy, near-woollen, layers of mist lying at ground level wrap themselves around the setting sun's golden halo. The grass, twinkling with dew, catches all the oblique, glancing rays of light. In our lungs, the wet, sweet-smelling earth, yet another delicate note to the pure air, adds to the enchantment.

We leave the leech forest and come onto a bitumen road leading to Yarrowitch, a small country town, which we avoid, to continue north. We return onto a dirt track, where, at a cattlegrid, I meet a father with his two children in a four-wheel drive. He's a charming man, with piercing blue eyes looking out from under the traditional bushman's hat. His little girl, Poppy, is seven years old. I tell them that I'm looking for Louise Clarke's property, which the Trail crosses. I explain that she has proposed to welcome us. Luck has it that he knows her; they're friends. I have his nearly four-year-old son ride Cooper and, as my adventure excites Poppy, I invite her to spend a day riding with me. In this area, children learn to ride almost as soon as they start to walk. Her father indicates a place for me and my horses to camp, and returns to drop by some steaks, beer and hay. Enough for everyone. Next morning, Poppy turns up on a big, grey horse, accompanied by her father, to spend the day with us and ride over to Louise Clarke's property. I love inspiring children's yearning for adventure and sharing my love of horses with them. I adore children and enjoy working with them in Aboriginal communities.

Louise Clarke, a cultured woman, is a well-known business coach. She shares her time between Sydney and the bush, where she applies holistic management to raising cattle in a sustainable way. After going around her property – and she's familiar with every nook and cranny of it – she takes me to see platypuses in a creek on her property. Their nature being very shy, I've never managed to see one in the flesh before. But, unfortunately, there are none around today.

Louise and her husband, Bill, welcome me warmly and invite me to stay in their home. This woman and her husband teach me many things about horses, in particular about the inconveniences and benefits of shoeing brumbies. She recommends books to read, several of which are about female personalities from the bush at a time when very little credit was given them. She knows Oxley Wild Rivers, the next park I will be going through, very well. It will be hard on my horses' hooves, she tells me, because of the number of rocky riverbeds. She insists on shoeing Cooper as he doesn't have any boots left, and Bill proposes shoeing my horses' forelegs himself. I'm not entirely convinced by this solution. I'm wavering, but their expert advice is persuasive, and I accept.

So our newly shod cavalry sets off for a park named after the English explorer John Oxley, who tried to go down the Macleay River, which crosses the park. It was World Heritage listed by UNESCO in 1994, in homage to its tropical forests and its rich biodiversity. Between the northern plateau and the east coast, its fourteen waterfalls, its spectacular gorges and its numerous rivers – like the Apsley and the Kunderang – all make this untamed territory into a new Eden. Nine hundred rare indigenous species proliferate here, among which are dozens of eucalypts, acacias, red cedars, and orchids and ferns that grow as epiphytes on the trunks of the great trees. I was warned against poisonous plants, however; their leaves and stalks are covered with fine hairs that can create painful burns, which could drive my companions crazy.

These thousands of hectares are a wild paradise. Loggers hunting for red cedars were the first white men to step into these spectacular canyons and lost valleys. Then, in the 1840s, risking perilous trips, cattle were brought in by drovers to graze in new pastures; following this, huts were built.

Colonisation drew near but didn't succeed in conquering all of this rugged immensity.

After our rest at Louise's, and once my horses are partially shoed, the young Poppy, hooked by our expedition, wants to ride with us for another day. This time, we happen to face a difficult trek, descending into a very steep gorge. We start tackling the vertical slope by winding our way down, and for hours Poppy follows on gamely until we reach the shelter planned for the night. With her father, she leaves me at that point, to return by daylight. The children of the bush thoroughly impress me.

Returning to my solitude, I build a big fire in the hut, which illuminates the old wooden shelter. Then, I sit outside under the stars, leaning against a stump. Eight days in this green ocean brings you back to your human roots and your place in nature. To the horses' delight, water and grass are in abundance, and I also take my fill of chlorophyl. Clouds of butterflies, concerts of birdsong, creepers running down venerable trees – life exultant.

I swim with my horses. In our camp, I hang out naked or in a sarong, alone in the universe. It's 27 degrees Celsius during the day, and cool at night. The ideal climate. On our way down vales and slopes, when we cross deep rivers, Cooper has taken it into his head to roll himself in the water – even when it's his turn to be the packhorse. I'm relieved that I was convinced to shoe them. The innumerable rocky, wide river crossings are extremely hard on their feet. Their surefootedness and resilience never cease to amaze me. I notice wild boar tracks around us. The herds are at home. A large lizard stares at us, gripping a tree trunk. Her body merges with the colour of the bark. She's a bearded dragon of the east and goes by the name *Pogona barbata* in Latin. As I venture into this untouched world, which I discover more of each day, it seems to nourish me, curing me of all my youthful negligence and carelessness.

A new hut, entirely built in green corrugated iron supposed to withstand fires, awaits us. I pick a bunch of yellow flowers to decorate this fleeting home, which is surrounded by traces of bushfires. The blackened trees, with their twisted and spiralled branches, seem to cry out their suffering. In his book *The Hidden Life of Trees*, the writer and forester Peter Wohlleben reveals that 'trees experience pain and have memories and that tree parents live together with their children …' But what do I know about the millions of mushrooms, insects, microorganisms that nourish, enrich and give life to the soil's humus and to the labyrinth of roots, without which there would be no trees – or practically anything? My ignorance of these secret and mysterious combinations morphs into curiosity. Wohlleben's book has me diving into an elusive and strange world that the ancient Celtic druids probably knew better than we do.

After these idyllic days, we're progressing towards the end of gorge country, on our way to the Macleay. We have a plunging view of the river, one of the main waterways of New South Wales. It can, in a few minutes, become impassable because of the number of its tributaries. All the paths are rocky, and water is everywhere, which forces me to walk rather than ride most of the time. At one point, Cooper shies away from something that has frightened him and lands all his 500 kilograms on my foot. Ouch.

I help a hiker to cross the Macleay, with all his gear, by putting him bareback on River, who's at rest for the day. The rocky riverbed is covered with plants that float like yellow lentils on the water. The layered greens of the vegetation surround us, with sporadic rocks of sandstone. On the water's edge, pines, eucalypts, and yellow-flowering bushes are encircled by a crown of mountains – and this whole spectacle is mirrored by the river. I swim with my horses – horses are natural swimmers – in the Macleay. It's such a joy after hours on foot.

I meet Neil, a nearby farmer, astride a brumby. I contacted him as we're going through his land. His property abuts the

The journey begins

Over thirteen long and gruelling months I travelled 5330 kilometres from the south to the north of Australia with my three horses: Roxanne, River and Cooper. Cat Vinton, an English photographer, joined us for a portion of the journey, observing and capturing the bond between me and my companions. I am so grateful to Cat for these memories of both the incredible highs of the trek, and the challenging lows.

Fox, my best friend and confidant, is not getting any younger.
When his arthritis flares up on humid days I carry him or put him
on my saddle. He never likes to show his pain, but I can tell.

Right

Travelling along mountain
peaks is exhausting but the
views are breathtaking.

Cat takes a spin in a helicopter to get a few aerial shots of the path ahead.

Crossing Mowbray River in Queensland.

Brumbies, considered a pest by the Australian government, are inquisitive and big-hearted animals. I share a bond with my three companions that is unlike anything else.

Water, grass and shade are my three priorities when choosing where to set up camp. Each day I create an ephemeral home in the bush – a sheepskin thrown over a log serves as an armchair in front of the fire.

Camping by the beach with my
horses is a dream come true.
I feel like Robinson Crusoe.

After long stretches on red dirt roads, it's a joy to travel along the coast.

On rest days I unburden the horses of their packs and let them canter freely along the beach.

Time for a late-afternoon drink.

Riding for six to eight hours a day takes its toll and I require high doses of medication to ease the pain.

A beautiful waterhole makes a nice change from bucket bathing.

During times of exhaustion,
the beauty of the bush
always gives me strength.

It's hard not to become emotional when we near the end of our journey. I thank my heroes – my brumbies – who have supported me throughout our trek.

Oxley Wild Rivers National Park. He offers me shelter in a hut on the edge of the park. He explains that, here, one can only muster the cattle on a horse; no vehicle can penetrate the canyon. He loves local brumbies. He trains them and puts them to work on his farm. His brumbies are well used to the rocky paths and, in spite of not having shoes, their feet are in perfect nick. Riding one of them, I'll spend a day helping Neil muster others who have escaped into the national park.

Four days out from arriving at Ebor – more of a hamlet than a village, with its 160 souls – we're gaining altitude. We climb to 1300 metres. It's been raining for three days. The temperature is falling. All my equipment is wet, and getting heavier each day. I can smell autumn in the air. On the last day, we travel 15 kilometres down a motorway, and the cars give us a generous splash every time they overtake us.

To give us a break, Erica has organised a truck for us in Dorrigo, where we lived and trained prior to starting the Trail. It's a small town of a thousand inhabitants, on a 770-metre-high plateau, surrounded by forests with outcrops of boulders. Here, I have a bed and shower – an amazing luxury. My three companions are showing signs of friction and pressure on their backs. I'm keen for them to enjoy a well-deserved rest, so they can recover. Dorrigo is near Ebor and Guy Fawkes

River National Park. This is my horses' cradle. On the 24th of April, Ebor signals the end of Section 8 in my guide book. The BNT is cut in slices, like a French *saucisson*. I've been heading up the Trail for 160 days and I'm not even halfway.

7

Brutal Splendours

Section 7: Ebor to Killarney

368 kilometres

10 May to 3 June 2016

Ten days' break in Erica's home does us a world of good. Roxanne, River and Cooper take a holiday in a large paddock – the very one in which I trained them. The vet examines my companions and gives them their vaccine shots. I fuss over them and add supplements to their diet every day, preparing for our return to nomadic life. We also check their backs.

I manage to escape to see the ocean, my favourite place in the world: that's where I replenish myself. I spent my childhood on an island in the Atlantic Ocean off the south-west coast of France – l'Île de Ré. As a result, I enjoy the waves, the tides, the smell of seaweed more than anything, and the cold water doesn't bother me.

I won't be crossing Guy Fawkes River National Park alone. The Sydney production company, who'd previously joined me on the Trail, will meet us. But this isolated park is inaccessible by vehicle – they are also prohibited – and involves a lot of planning; Erica is organising it. The film crew will catch up with us on horseback during the five days we'll spend in the Guy Fawkes National Park. Three members of the crew will be present – Gisela, Carlston and a sound guy – as well as three members of the Guy Fawkes Heritage Horse Association: Erica, Graeme, and my friend Kate. Owning a few Guy Fawkes brumbies herself, Kate and I became good friends during my months of planning for the trek. Twelve horses are necessary for conveying the food, gear, water and filming equipment, without forgetting a few drinks, like whiskey. Our horses are all brumbies, without exception, from the Guy Fawkes River National Park; all trained by Erica, Graeme and Kate. I'm excited to return to these magnificent landscapes that I only have a surface knowledge of. They shelter about two thousand wild horses. For my brumbies, it's almost a homecoming after a long absence. They're returning to their native land.

I'm surprised and touched that the association has organised an open day to support my expedition, to help with my horses' veterinarian bills. The expenses, by this point, have emptied my savings, and I'm now having to live off credit from my bank. The day turns out to be a success, thanks to the two hundred visitors. The participants are curious and ask a lot of questions. They're impressed by Roxanne's, River's and Cooper's good physical condition after six months on the Trail. I'm grateful to Erica for putting on the event and for her support.

It is the 9th of May, and we've travelled 1977 kilometres. Two of the reputedly hardest sections of the 5330-kilometre Trail are behind us, but the road to the end is still long – the slightest weakening is out of the question. More than ever before, I try to keep my goal in sight. Autumn is here. I'm mentally preparing myself for winter. I leave Dorrigo for the Guy Fawkes River National Park, about 50 kilometres away. There, I'm supposed to meet Erica and the film crew in two or three days. This exceptional park of over 100,000 hectares is a rugged river gorge with grey rock faces, and forests that can only be crossed on horseback. It counts more than forty different communities of vegetation, twenty-eight of which are endangered species; twenty-four of its species of animals are also endangered. Large swathes of these ancient forests are highly protected. River valleys and abyssal gorges follow an old geological fault line. The Trail runs along the western shore of the river and the only existing paths are created by wild horses' hooves, called 'brumby pads'. The river owes its name to Major Edward Parke, who, in 1845, camped nearby on the 5th of November – Guy Fawkes Day in England.

At night especially, the higher we go, the cold starts setting in. The brumbies' coats have changed: they're getting thicker. So my horses are also preparing themselves for winter, to fight against the icy morning winds. We continue moving. It takes three days before we can reach Erica and the film crew. To make progress in the park with twelve horses will turn out to be a complex operation. At the first beautiful panorama, the film crew comes to a halt. All the equipment must be taken out of the pack saddlebags, then the filming takes place, then everything must be packed away again before we can leave.

We're mesmerised to see such beautiful scenery with wild horses moving freely in their natural habitat. My three companions and I remain patient, even tolerant. I see my favourite shrubs, the *Xanthorrhoea glauca*, nicknamed *black-boys* by my Aboriginal friends or *grass trees*. A kind of tree trunk capped with a shaggy headdress of stalks, the grass tree is capable of living for up to six hundred years – quite a performance. When this tree is burnt, it looks like a human being, with its smooth trunk supporting a head. It was used as food, as drink, and also as a building material. No less than twenty-eight different species of this versatile, all-purpose tree exist.

Erica doesn't stop to take a breath. She makes food, prepares the fire to cook the meats, pours bourbon. She's everywhere. The advantage of a short trip of five days is being able to take a lot of equipment along. We visit a hut, during a short stop, and it transports us into the past. The presence of the horses and all the gear on their backs could lure us into believing that we're back in the days of the gold-diggers and settlers. The savage beauty of this park is unique, as are the species and variety of hues of the plant life. The smooth-barked Australian oaks, so different from European ones, grow freely. Because of the absence of paths to safely cross the river, instead we follow tracks created by animals. As we descend into the gorge, my companions prick up their ears. They're getting antsy – they know where they are. After a long moment goes by, we catch sight of a group of young buckskin and bay colts, in great physical condition and with solid muscles. Surprised by us, as inquisitive as cats, they prance around, their tails and noses raised. My guys are in a state; talking to them, I reassure them.

That night at the bivouac, worried, I camp near my companions. The film crew's horses have their own enclosure. Erica, Graeme, Kate and I take it in turns through the night to keep an eye on our mounts. During the day, we progress slowly. I feel compelled to adapt to the film crew's requirements, to respect their rhythm. We don't have a day's rest; usually, two, three days of travelling would be followed by a twenty-four-hour break. The river flows in a gorge lined with yellow-orange grasses. We thread our way through a pine forest, where nourishing grass, for our horses, is scarce. One night, we observe, from our camp, the fantastic spectacle of a herd of about fifty brumbies. In five days, we must have seen about two hundred of them romping around in the wilderness; among them many palominos, buckskins and greys.

On the 15th of May, I tick off our 180th day on the Trail, as I step out of Guy Fawkes River National Park with Roxanne, River and Cooper. We reach Newton Boyd, was once home to a small community of cattle breeders before they caved-in to the extreme isolation, by an ordinary road. An old school, and a few derelict fences remain, and a mob of unmanaged domestic horses in very poor condition linger on in the ghost settlement. A war memorial, a last vestige of the past, reminds onlookers of the soldiers from around here who fought in the trenches.

At the end of the afternoon, the Guy Fawkes association members and the film crew leave us. I enjoyed sharing this experience with Erica, Graeme and Kate, but I'm relieved about the film crew's departure as their filming requirements were very detrimental to my team's travelling pace. I'm gathering wood for the fire when a trail-bike rider stops by for 'a little chat'. He's looking for a place to camp. He looks nice, with his wide smile and his beard. I propose to share my bivouac. I've only met him five minutes ago, but I feel I can trust him. When you're travelling day in and day out, you learn to listen to your intuition about those you meet on the road. You have to take risks to make discoveries. Gordon is an eccentric Englishman and a big, hefty guy. He has built up a removal business in Byron Bay. With his wife, a social worker, he has two children. We drink 'to friendship' and, after a few whiskeys, Gordon starts singing like a crooner. He wants to bring one of his children for a day on the Trail with me. Then possums intervene and start pilfering our saddlebags. *Pirates!* We run after them and Gordon suggests catching one and turning him on the spit over the fire. I give up the chase – I'm not so keen to eat possum meat. Using our saddlebags as pillows, we fall asleep under the stars, each on one side of the fire, after having killed a bottle of whiskey. In the middle of the night, Gordon, stark naked, gets up to add some wood

to the embers, yelling at me not to turn around. Too late. I
chuckle and fall back to sleep.

After ten days of travel without a single day's rest and
a dearth of feed, I stop in a cattle reserve, with a 100-acre
paddock at our disposal. There, my trio can be free to chew
grass to their hearts' content. Running, I go in search of water.
The horses follow me at a trot – free. I really have the feeling
of belonging to their herd. On my rest day, I'm so tired that
I hardly make it out of my sleeping bag. The horses keep
checking on me, begging me for a treat. I share everything
with them, to Fox's disgust.

In the next section of the Trail, the cold catches up with me.
Isolated, I follow old cattle tracks, west of Gibraltar Range
National Park. I'm due to arrive at a property belonging to
the Petit family. They'll shelter me in a hut with an adjacent
cistern: happiness, near-luxury. Considering the cold, I sleep
in front of the fire on a camp bed, with a view of the moon
through the window in front of me. In the morning, I still
have a few more embers on my fire and I make my coffee
from my bed. What more can you ask? This comfort is so
welcome and appreciated, however rustic. A few sunbeams

stream in via the window. The air is still very fresh. There has even been some frost in the night. I love the smell of the fire, and of the coffee, of course – I can't function without a coffee. Roxanne pokes her head through the door, as if to say, 'Hurry up!'

In Washpool National Park, the four-wheel-drive path peters out into a cattle track. We find ourselves in a very isolated valley along the banks of the Rocky River. At night, my tent is covered in frost. Grass is becoming scarce, but at least the water from the river is at hand and the pine forests surround us protectively. It's a relentless couple of weeks, which I navigate completely alone. With each page, the details in the Trail guide grow more and more random, and the distances approximate at best. 'Follow the river the best you can,' it advises at one point, unashamedly.

My objective is to reach Billirimba Station on Demon Creek. A fault line forms a perfect corridor following the National Trail. Kathryn and Preston warned me that the property owner was of the *grumpy* variety: kindness and welcome weren't his forte, and he wouldn't look kindly on Fox. In this area, private properties are crossed through padlocked doors. Passage must be wrangled with the owners, and it's not a foregone conclusion. I am a tad anxious at the prospect of meeting him; his presence is heralded by a line of washing drying outside his house. I prefer to camp near a stream on the edge of this land. There is very little for my horses to graze on, and we're dead-beat. I'm about to heat up my miserable dinner, when the man turns up in a cattle truck, with an intimidating look on his face. But then he mellows and presses me to leave my brumbies, inviting me to come and warm up and have dinner at his place. He takes some meat out and asks me to cook it for us. I learn that his wife has just died of cancer and that, as it turns out, a little company would do him good.

After three frosty mornings of finding Roxanne, River and Cooper shaking when I wake up, I'm very keen for a few days' rest. I've picked up a cold myself; with the exhaustion and sore muscles it feels a lot worse than usual. Our path crosses a motorway. Here, the camp site has a hut and fenced paddock. I take this opportunity to lift my thumb and get a ride to go find some food. Thanks to my SPOT tracker and to social media, a German woman who has followed my adventure assiduously proposes to come and pick me up. She invites me to have a shower at her place and makes a soup to perk me up. I leave my companions at the TSR paddock, so that they can relax and graze around, free. My host also owns some brumbies, and plans on adopting more from the Guy Fawkes association. She used to live in Byron Bay. Then, when her husband died, she decided to move to this wild area, where she also practises equine therapy.

Ten days after my meeting with Gordon, the well-built Englishman, he returns with his son, Harvey, who's eleven years old. I put Harvey on Cooper, the one with whom he bonded last time. For six hours, this young boy keeps up with us perfectly, while his father takes charge of transporting the pack equipment in his truck – a holiday for my little team. Arriving at camp, I discover that Gordon has brought a whole load of furniture in his removalist's truck. He positions an enormous sofa in front of a huge bonfire and undertakes to grill some sausages, after offering me a beer. His eccentricity, kindness and laughter warm the cockles.

We're two days from Killarney. The township sits in the middle of a green valley surrounded with dark green, nearly black, round-topped mountains. The road is taking me to Queensland. The weather is cold and grey. A large wire fence marks the border between New South Wales and Queensland, the second-largest state in Australia, three times the size of France. I don't let this daunt me. The wire fence is to avoid invasion by rabbits carrying myxomatosis, a scourge introduced by humans with the intention of decimating the prolific rabbit population, which was destroying both crops and flora. It's the recurring story of the sorcerer's apprentice: now, myxomatosis has spread throughout the country, creating havoc, and even attacking breeders' rabbits.

Although I'm arriving in the 'Sunshine State', it's winter, and I'm wearing thermals and woollen tights at night. The cold is my worst enemy. But during the day the weather is good in these partly tropical latitudes.

Queensland is the state with the longest portion of the Trail. It has three vast regions. I have learnt that in the south and in the centre are large, cattle-rich, agricultural areas of bananas and sugar cane, as well as mining resources – mainly coal. The north, sparsely populated and difficult to access, basks in a tropical climate and reaches to a sea of coral. I'm preparing myself for the poisonous animals that abound, like snakes and spiders, but also the Ross River mozzies, which transmit fevers or epidemic polyarthritis. Without forgetting the crocodiles, and a few others …

We're crossing the frontier and I can see Killarney in front of us! High as a kite without a drop of beer, I holler and start galloping. Wrong impulse – the presence of llamas in a field stuns my horses, who have never clapped eyes on a llama. Not recognising my voice because of my excitement, they start side-stepping and rearing, ready to bolt. I'm on the verge of being unseated and thrown to the ground. Afterwards, a bit rattled, I park my horses at the rodeo grounds with some hay, and I reach the pub, where a few beers help to settle me. I find a farrier, who comes to fit new shoes on my horses. It's crucial to keep on top of my horses' shoeing needs and to organise a farrier to meet us every five to six weeks to replace them, making sure to avoid any trouble in more remote areas. I also expend effort in feeding the horses extra pellets, and add some healthy provisions for myself in the bargain: a precaution that will keep us all in good shape.

I'm getting ready to go, a coffee in hand, when Damian, my ex-husband, with whom I shared so many adventures, turns up. We haven't seen each other for a couple of years, but we've stayed good mates. He's a bit like my brother in spirit. He's going to follow me for a while on foot and film us. Together, we have ridden in Mongolia; crossed India on motorbikes, and China by train; travelled more than 10,000 kilometres on a motorbike with our gear in its sidecar, from Lake Baikal, in Siberia, to France; lived for a year on a remote peninsula of Bahia, in Brazil; and worked in Aboriginal communities. After so many adventures, a strong connection remains between us. With Damian, life is easy – we shared so many things that everything is simple between us.

8
Queensland, a Mental Challenge

Section 6: Killarney to Blackbutt

393 kilometres

7 June to 29 June 2016

After the rain, the sun … I'm touched that Damian should come to find me. Even if I haven't seen him for two years, our bond is still there. We're following hills now, the foothills of the Great Dividing Range running along the east coast.

Tonight, contrary to my usual early bedtime, we stay staring out silently into the night, near the fire. A while later, Damian disappears to water a tree. I feel my spirit loosening from its bonds and setting itself free to float and wander. Suddenly it feels so dark – for once, I light my torch. A snake is sliding between my legs. A ten-thousand-volt surge of adrenalin has me leaping to my feet. Pure instinct makes me grab a piece of wood and push my deadly visitor onto the embers. Tough and spunky, it fights back several times. It takes all my energy to fling it into the flames, at last. When Damian runs back, he can't believe it's all over, bar the shouting. We watch the reptile, smoking in its death throes, exuding a revolting smell, writhing and thrashing. It finally curls into the flame. The pattern on the scales collapses into accordion-folds in the ashes. It was a close shave. Had she bitten me, had Damian not been there, I wouldn't have been long for this world. I'm mostly abandoned to my own mercies here; any help, miles away. My vigilance mustn't falter. This reality is to be kept in mind at all times, but without letting it grow into a phobia. The Trail is littered with snakes – I must live with it.

The immensity of this state, with its gigantic properties, is dawning on me. The National Trail could become more monotonous, though, with the landscape spreading without pause right up to the horizon. I foresee the boredom of infinite flat lands and infinite flat plains ahead. The challenge isn't a physical one anymore – it's a mental one. I've come to a turning point in my personal adventure.

The vegetation has changed. We're going through forests of grass trees. We enter Condamine, a name that has a French sound to it. The gorge frames the eponymous river, an apparently peaceful river, flowing between grassy verges, planted with trees bending romantically over the water. Only there's a hidden bombshell in this utopian picture: in 2016, an environmentalist member of parliament set this river on fire, demonstrating that the water contained bubbles of methane. According to the activist, this is one of the damaging consequence of the hydrofracturing, or fracking, of shale to produce gas and petrol. The shocking photos and videos show the surface of the Condamine River alive with flames. It was a disturbing demonstration.

In Rosevale, the next stop, we meet a farmer and his English wife, who kindly give us shelter. I'm so grateful and humbled by this chain of solidarity and hospitality – like at sea or in the desert. Damian follows on foot. He walks next to my horses, and we cross the Cunningham Highway, which runs from west to east in this region, a precious umbilical cord. After spending three weeks in the bush, the return to civilisation feels more odd to me than it does usually. In a paddock on the foothills of the Great Divide, under the setting sun, we savour beers bought from a local farmer, and taste the dusk. The sky is golden, bespattered with a few glittering clouds of blushing pink and orange. Damian makes his small video, a sketch of my daily life on the Trail.

The more we move up north the warmer it gets, as we approach the equator. Humidity and heat – everything is growing rapidly, with the unhoped-for rain of the last three days. After the weather of the past weeks, my brumbies are still wearing their winter coats, which must now be uncomfortable for them. We're moving along a narrow valley, flanked by mountains. At the end of the week, Damian goes away again, carrying a provision of videos. His departure leaves a vacuum, and I bivouac without human company again, near a vegetable farm. The farm owner gives me some cauliflower, cherry tomatoes and a broccoli: I'm so grateful – this fresh fare is a delight.

The next day, in a landscape strewn with pink-flowered cactuses, I meet Eliza and her daughter, Zaydee, with their donkeys. The BNT coordinator shelters us all together with our mounts. Thanks to her, we can camp on the edge of a village.

For a few days, we travel separately – our animals don't progress at the same rhythm – meeting up at night. We travel through Ravensbourne National Park's magnificent rainforest, the perfect model for a tropical forest, only a little part of which would have been preserved. In the past, these forests of gigantic trees covered the whole region – this was before human intervention. We camp under the awning of a sportsground and our conversation moves on to our very different approaches to travel. Comparing experiences is always enlightening. At another moment in time, on a private property, we share for the span of a night a wood-and-brick hut, where antlers, hanging on the wall, throw the most surrealist shadow and remind me of my father's home. Zaydee has fallen in love with Cooper; in the end, our horses seem to get on rather well. Because of the lack of grass, we buy supplements from the farmers according to our needs.

During one weekend, I take the leap and decide to participate in a carnival of polocrosse, the Stanley Rivers Carnival, happening very close to the Trail path. I make sure my three companions are in a safe place and head off for my first experience of this type of sport. Fast, fun, exacting and competitive, it's very different from classical polo, which demands six horses from each contestant, making it a sport exclusively reserved for contestants with well-lined pockets. In polocrosse, the competition is focused on skill and strategy. Only one mount is allowed, with the idea of encouraging the player to preserve its energy and wellbeing. The rider has a lacrosse stick – a racket with a net at the end of a long, supple stick. We must catch a ball with it. The speed is essentially at a gallop, and I find myself astride a large, well-trained horse named Charlie Brown. He has been lent to me, and he charges at lightning-speed – a real tank. We form such a good team that I bring another rider to the ground, who comes out of it with three broken ribs. Poor fellow – I feel terrible! Two teams out of three compete, with three other players as reserve riders. The teams are mixed, with both men and women together. Mine has a white and green bib. We play twice for twenty minutes each time. At the end of the game, I receive a bag of pellets for my brumbies – a useful prize. I have had fun and, happily, have copped no wounds.

I return to the Trail, alone again with my three friends. I decide to bivouac next to a little stream. It's cold and there's a lot of wind. I'm lucky to have the sleeping bag Erica gave me in the Guy Fawkes River National Park. Around midnight, in a deep sleep, I'm woken by the sound of bells. My three companions are restless. Then, I hear the sound of them at full gallop; they've got out of their enclosure. In spite of their hobbles, they've managed to jump the enclosure. Something I didn't sense has frightened them. Horses don't like the wind; their hearing is vastly more sensitive than ours. I'm fumbling in pitch darkness and walk towards the sound of the bells, barefooted and without a torch. I call them as I move in their direction. I tell them I'm coming to them, so they're expecting me. I speak to them, reassure them, calm them in the inky night, by touch. I unstrap their hobbles, bring them back to camp, and set about reassembling their enclosure, before returning to bed, relieved, for a few hours. Luckily my voice reassures them when they're frightened.

In the morning, we set off on a dirt track. Thirty curious horses follow us through a paddock. Just before reaching Blackbutt, a wood-industry town, which saw the gold-panning fever at the end of the 1800s, Gordon the Englishman and his son, Harvey, turn up – Harvey wants to ride Cooper again. Once I've settled my crew at the Blackbutt rodeo ground, I visit an op shop, because most of my clothes are in tatters. After Blackbutt, Eliza, Zaydee and I are happy to spend a day on the Trail together. Gordon follows us in his four-wheel drive. Zaydee rides River bareback, and Harvey rides Cooper again. My brumbies are as good as gold with a child on their back. As for the kids, it's a long day's ride and they are healthily exhausted.

9
Cutting a Bit of Slack in Biggenden

Section 5: Blackbutt to Biggenden

313 kilometres

30 June to 20 July 2017

Every five weeks, to ward off problems, I organise an appointment with a farrier. I've planned to provide my brumbies with thick metal shoes with titanium nails to protect their hooves and save their feet. Erica's son, who is himself a farrier, helps me find a skilled farrier in the region, which isn't easy. 'Operation Horseshoe' takes place in Nanango, an old Queensland locale that was once inhabited by Indigenous people of the Wakka Wakka tribe and is now the domain of sheep and dairy-cow breeders, and also, in a minor way, of the wood industry. I camp on the Elgin Vale property, inside an old sawmill. We're close to some swamps, and I see black swans – always a shock for someone coming from a land of white swans – stags and innumerable species of birds. An Australian king parrot pays me a visit, his bright red-and-green feathers on royal display. I meet the women in the village school, who've seen my brumbies and want to know more about them. They ask me to share in their meal.

The Country Women's Association of Australia is a very large association, created in 1926 by Mary Jane Warnes, who was considered an activist at a time when women's rights were limited. Founded to help women in rural communities to lead better lives, this association is present all over Australia. Very active during the 1929 'Crash' and during World War II, they provided clothing and food for those in need. They also participated in the war effort by sewing camouflage gear for the soldiers.

Those members who invited me to lunch are preparing food for their yearly meeting in the community school – each person brings something. One of them explains to me that, with the passage of time, this group may not be so active today as it once was. Due to the growth of different forms of media and access to transport, she adds, the association has lost many of its members. She believes that the younger generation doesn't have the desire to stay in these remote places. Anyway, the lunch is instructive, and delicious for a nomad so used to sketchy meals.

Later, when I've settled in the old sawmill with all my equipment, in the middle of the night, a great chill and fatigue seizes me. I can't breathe. It's still dark when I get up. It's the 6th of July and I feel that my body is packing up. Exhausted after nearly seven months on the Trail, I stuff myself with all the vitamins of the alphabet.

This day, the 7th of July, I light a fire to heat up a can of baked beans, which doesn't happen often; I usually content myself with nuts and biscuits. My forays into cooking do not venture very far, but I need to eat something hot. I'm covered with layers of clothing: practically all I have with me. I hadn't expected Queensland to still be so cold.

After a long day, we reach a lake. There's a bit of grass. I decide to install our camp. An old van is already parked there. Disappointed to have to share the spot, I see two men coming out of the vehicle; one of them is older, with a beard. I've no choice; it's the only grass I can find. I set up about 10 metres away from them, unravel my three companions' enclosure and we start to chat. They offer me some of their sausages: 'Thank you, that's kind of you …' I say. I'm not interested in their joints, though; I've got a long day ahead of me and the next-morning after-effects are never rosy. Contrary to my first impression, these two men turn out to be original and interesting. We spend a great evening.

The guy with the beard starts playing the guitar and then the saxophone. He plays old jazz tunes, and his outfit is hilarious: sunglasses in the middle of the night, a long grey beard, a camouflage beanie, a black leather jacket, and ugg boots on his feet. Quite a look ... I can't help myself from taking a photograph of this memorable travelling character, living in his van and writing poetry in the heart of the bush.

Kilkivan, traditional lands of the Gubbi Gubbi, was settled by Europeans in the 1840s. The village has a lot of character, as its well-restored old buildings attest. An old lady named Dawn offers to welcome me into her home – another nice surprise. I also take part in one of this village's events: a campdraft show. This unique Australian sport involves a horse and rider working in tandem to separate a beast from the herd, as well as a lot of horse sales.

There I meet Rosie. In her fifties, she has a bed and breakfast in her lovely colonial Queenslander house. She generously offers me room and board and cooks me delicious meals. This open, welcoming woman is part of an organisation called the Kilkivan Great Horse Ride, which holds a parade on horseback every year. This big event happens in April, attracting up to a thousand riders and their horses to Kilkivan. Located along the Trail, this village saw one of its founders, Reginald Murray 'RM' Williams as he's more commonly known, marching down the main street, in their 1988 parade for one of the official inaugurations of this colossal trek.

The Trail follows the old carriageway. The terrain is rather flat, and provides space for cattle pastures. Then come a succession of state-forest paths, where I only meet woodcutters. But there's no grass among the underwood, and vegetation is scarce. A certain routine sets in. In the middle of the forest, I bivouac in a Scout camp where the pastor allows me to stop. There, I had organised a hay-drop to help my friends to get through this section containing very little feed. It's lashing rain, which hasn't happened for a long time, and I take shelter under an awning. These last few days, I've felt cut-off and quite alone in the universe. This grieving, this haunting by absent friends and family comes on suddenly, without warning. The life I'm leading is taking its toll and I never know when my world is going to lose its moorings, in danger of being swamped by the immensity of the larger world surrounding us.

I find the Mary River littered with debris and heaps of tree trunks from the floods. On the other shore, it's a jungle: reeds and dense vegetation obstruct the river and make it difficult to cross. After a reccy, I manage to find a spot covered with an intertwining network of large ficus roots, on which we can tread to reach the other side. I stumble upon an old hippie, who's built himself a house in the trees, and we salute each other; he must have a lot of opportunities for meditation in his nest.

I continue on my way. Some inquisitive cows are following us. Are they intending to follow the Trail? We camp near a sign, the first one I have encountered on the whole trek. It gives the distance from our departure point in Healesville as 2978 kilometres. That's quite a distance, but there's still nearly as much to go. These figures depress me completely. It's the 14th of July, Bastille Day, and we've been seven months and twenty-seven days on the Trail. I'm starting to lose all notion of time. I'm not even sure if this should be a day of rejoicing for me. I visualise in a flash the whole trek we have ahead of us before reaching Cooktown, our arrival point at the very north end of Queensland. I may well be halfway to achieving the goal I set myself as a challenge, but tonight I feel overwhelmed. The water has a swampy taste: my filter is jammed, and I have nothing to drink. As luck has it, people passing by in a four-wheel drive help me out with a few litres. But my horses haven't had anything to eat.

We find ourselves on the only connecting path through this immense and often impenetrable bush, where, in spite of the solitude surrounding the Trail, here and there I make interesting, quite unique, acquaintances with men and women. Sometimes they appear just at the right moment, as if sent by destiny. This very day, when everything seems to be going haywire, I meet a bushman, Len, in his fifties, and his niece, Sharon. Very welcoming, they propose to host me at their place. The invitation couldn't come at a better time. There is a social life on the Trail, as I have experienced since I began on this adventure. When I leave Len and Sharon, as I'm riding along with my three companions, I see a very scrawny horse, all skin and bones, padlocked inside a large fenced ground, totally abandoned, in the middle of nowhere. Not a house to be seen. I alert the RSPCA.

When I reach Biggenden, one of those small places that seems to come straight out of the American West, with its main street flanked by low houses, and large electric poles with bunches of tangled wires hanging from them. My only thought is to buy, beg or steal some hay – my cavalry is hungry. Then, I find a rodeo ground to camp in, where I can have some hay delivered. We have a magnificent view of Mount Walsh. I get to the pub on horseback, like in the good old times; but, seeing as progress is unstoppable, I buy some beers, from atop my horse, from the drive-through counter: a shop where one is served in one's car or on one's horse in a queue that echoes that of a freeway tollbooth. Later, after a delectable shower, I crash in my camp. Perked up by the hot water and my rest, I organise two visits – one to the retirement home and the other to the school. I want to raise awareness of the brumbies' plight in Australia and share my love for these extraordinary, resilient and multi-talented horses.

On the path leading to the retirement home, I stop for a wonderful breakfast, including a double ration of bacon for Fox, in a delightful open-air cafe. I find an inviting small, round table and metal chair. Roxanne doesn't fail to beg for food, just behind me. For the cafe owners, this isn't quite a common occurrence. At the retirement home, flanked by Roxanne, River and Cooper, my visit is a rare, joyful moment for the older people, some of whom are nearly a hundred or more. I stand facing row upon row of lined and storied faces in the audience. Many are wheelchair-bound. They all want to pat my brumbies and have their photograph taken with them. A ninety-year-old man, who appears very frail in his wheelchair, is desperate to touch them – and when he does, his smile is a gift. Since my last visit, one lady has hung a souvenir photo taken with River in her room and calls me regularly to get news about him.

On this occasion, the benefits of equine therapy appear evident. I'm convinced of the extent to which it can help people recover their zest for life. Horses have the innate capacity to bring peace to those they come into contact with, as well as piquing their interest and breaking their routines of existence. My three travel companions stay docile, and lend themselves gently to my experiment. For those who may be very lonely, they create memories, and genuine moments of joy and tenderness.

At the school, the children that I seat on Roxanne are in ecstasies. In front of the group of kids, assembled by their teacher, I give a little talk about my expedition. I underline for them, and often insist on, the talents and qualities of this ancient breed of wild horses, who are subject to much controversy and are still frowned upon by many Australians.

Biggenden signals the end of Section 5. After my outings to raise awareness, I use this juncture as an opportunity to take two days' rest. My companions heartily deserve it.

10

You're the Boss

I leave Biggenden village with three young girls, two of whom are barrel-racing champions: a competition involving riding as fast as possible around barrels without making any fall down – a kind of horse slalom. They are keen to ride with me on the trek for a day. Why not? I love the idea of supporting and inspiring their sense of adventure. A father and his daughter join us, too.

On the 24th of July, we're travelling to Paradise Dam on Burnett River, an enormous reservoir lake that entirely submerged a village dating back to the goldrush in 1885, from which it derives its name. A golden paradise that vanished like fairy dust when the vein dried up. That night, we camp along the Burnett's wide and rocky shore. Thinking my horses would not be able to cross the river and its steep shores, I don't set up their enclosure. In the morning, I call Roxanne, River and Cooper. For the first time since we started off, I receive no response. No sign of their presence, in spite of their hobbles; no sound of their bells, either. My anxiety skyrockets. I climb the ridge to look around, convinced that they couldn't have crossed the river with their hobbles. Nothing.

My world falls apart. I'm facing the worst thing that could happen to me: my horses have run away. I can hear no reassuring sound, nor detect the slightest trace of them. The horizon is empty, the silence total. I walk a couple of kilometres, on top of the ridge, searching for fresh dung and tracks, tears pouring down my face. My friends have never moved this far away from me. I return to camp, still calling them, when I hear a faint bell sound towards the water ... *Is it my imagination?* I wade across the river without much believing in what I have heard. But there isn't so much as a shadow of a mane. I retrace yesterday's leg of the Trail, in a kind of agony of despair. At last, miraculously, I see them from the top of a hill. They haven't wandered that far from our camp, but following their instinct they have situated themselves upwind of me, to where sound doesn't carry. I'm nearly dizzy with relief. The runaways look at me innocently – obviously at peace with their consciences. They have no idea of the torment they've subjected me to. I'm stunned they've managed to cross the river with their hobbles. The error of judgement is mine – I can only take it out on myself. Not a word of rebuke escapes me, but I promise myself, a bit late in the day perhaps, that it will never happen again.

We set off once more for Mount Perry valley, the highest mountain around here. It reminds me of the Vosges mountain range in France. The small village, named after the mountain, is nestled in the foothills, where goldmining is still active. I ask in the pub if there is anywhere I can shelter my horses. The publican allows me to put them in the enclosure at the back of his establishment, and gives me a room with mates rates. Children, sitting at a large table, are having tea on the pub's back terrace. Roxanne, River and Cooper gently move in closer. Nothing scares them. The mine staff who've come to drink their beers caress my companions, who are soon eating straight off the children's plates. If they could, they'd be eating at the table. After so many months on the road, my horses trust the humans they meet on the way. They've become a little human themselves – Roxanne licks the plates without a blink. A little while ago my two geldings only ate grass and hay. Their tastes have evolved.

A nine-year-old girl grabs the chance to skip a day of school and spends a day riding in our company. Her mother accompanies us on her own horse, her daughter on River's back. A small voice has been telling me for a few days that I'm getting behind on my schedule, considering the climate awaiting us in North Queensland. I'm taking the chance of arriving during the rain season, in extreme heat and in the midst of tropical storms, which would make the whole venture unworkable. I can't compete with nature. I'm not travelling fast enough and it's worrying me. Celebrating slowness has a price.

The streams have practically dried out on Wombah Road, and they're not really serviceable with cattle trampling through them. I erect our camp by a set of yards with a rainwater tank and a fenced paddock – an absolute luxury, which I don't normally indulge in without permission. Horses come to meet us. A table under a tree comes in useful. I lay out my equipment in the enclosure surrounding the yards; evidently, a private place. The spot is lovely. In the morning, Fox is at my side, still half asleep. He doesn't feel like moving at all. I'm sure he's wondering why we have to get up so early. I am too. It's still too cold at night. I've followed the bushmen's good advice and covered my sleeping bag with a fine, nylon tarp, which protects me and Fox from cold and humidity. I've also wrapped my head in a long scarf, which really works to ward off the chill. Queensland's temperatures are such a shock – so warm during the day and yet so chilly at night.

A few days later, on a winding dirt track, I meet Shane, whose friend Terry is a taxidermist, specialising in crocodiles. This has me smiling, considering the number of them wandering around in Queensland. Apart from his talent as a naturalist, Terry is off-the-grid, a free spirit, an outsider. This region, which is rife with large cattle stations, has been divided up into much smaller plots of land. These have been bought by eccentrics who live here in a very creative way, practically cut-off from the world – environmentalists, Robinson Crusoes who produce their own electricity with a solar panel, and are happy with a dash of rain.

I'm moving towards a camp location, while Shane has arranged for me to leave my companions on a neighbouring farmer's land. His friend Terry lived a long time in Cape York, the most northerly point of Queensland, teeming with the region's main raw material – crocodiles. With his wife and children, they've built their home with their own hands. The biggest building on his property, which he uses as his workshop, is his shed. This is where he toils on the enormous beasts with the impressive dentition: some are hanging from the ceiling, and a 5-metre one he is just finishing is on a table, frozen in time with its jaw wide open. Shane is a kind of artist, engraving and painting on skulls of all sorts – deer, dingos, cows. With the family and a few friends, we drink beer after beer, and they prepare a seafood lunch – a wonderful feast. Shane proffers his engraving talents, offering to give me a tattoo. A little worse for wear, we decide on a drawing: a feather on the inside of my left arm with the words 'Wild at Heart', surrounded with birds in flight. *Migration and travel.* This suits me down to the ground. Shane progresses infinitely slowly along my arm while I'm lying down on the kitchen table with Fox on my left, and a glass of red wine in my right hand. I'm not disappointed with the result. I love this image by an artist hidden on the margins of modern civilisation. Thank you, my friend.

The next day, the 31st of July, on a very hot road, my brumbies and I are climbing a hill. I'm walking by their side. A few cars overtake us at full speed, making us swallow clouds of dust. At the crossroad, towards midday, I stumble on a pleasant young man perched on a blue tractor. Something *different* seems to emanate from him. He greets me with a smile and wants to know if I'm the girl who's crossing Australia with her horses.

His name is Mitch. He explains that his mother, that very morning, showed him a video of my adventure from social media. He had been off on his vehicle to clear some bushes. The way he looks intrigues me. Firstly, he's barefoot, which I find attractive. He's got a beard, a cap, and very gentle, blue eyes. But then he asks me for one of my rollie cigarettes, which annoys me because they're so precious. We chat for five minutes and then he opens a gate for us that we have to get through. My horses and I continue on our way but, before we can get very far, Mitch overtakes us. *Do I need anything, and would I like to drink a beer with him at sundown? Absolutely. That would be really great.* I tell him I'll be camping on the edge of Kolan River, a few kilometres down the road. That's where he'll be able to find me. On the way, I realise that there are a few fords to cross. Just in case, I put up a sign: 'The girl with the horses, next ford'. He can't go wrong. After putting up my camp, I wait for the promised beer. Mitch plays hard-to-get, arriving late. However, rather than bringing one beer, he brings a whole carton of them. *Forgiven!* Night falls; we make a big fire as we pursue our lengthy discussions. He's still barefoot, and I notice how at home he is with nature. I learn that he's a helicopter pilot, but he doesn't boast about it. He's divorced, too. He's enjoying his job's itinerant lifestyle. We drink under the shooting starts – I count twenty-four. He teaches me how to find the Southern Cross. He leaves late, and the next morning, I curse him. It's so hard to get going with a hangover and on so little sleep.

Two days later, cognisant of my itinerary, Mitch catches up with me at the pub in Mungungo, a hundred-year-old establishment cooked in its own juices, with charming owners. I'm happy to see him, without deviating from my route: I must carry on.

My Trail companions and I ride between deep-green mountain ridges, like waves of stone. It's a splendid part of Kroombit Tops National Park, all hills in succession, and rocky cliffs covered in trees and high grasses. Unbelievable landscapes unravel as far as we can see, the temperature becoming cooler as we climb higher and higher. I'm on foot once again, following my friends. The rise and fall of the blue-veiled summits up here are a solid sea. This park is so immense that it took them fifty years to find the wreck of *Little Eva*, the American liberator bomber that disappeared at the end of World War II. From up here, I glimpse brumbies, and escaped cattle from private properties, which can sometimes be aggressive.

From wonder to wonder, we walk through the underbrush, rocked by the wind. I no longer tie up my horses when I dismount to do something, which requires a solid dose of trust. The three of them wait for me peacefully, while I make videos of the pure poetry of our surroundings. I thank them with small gifts of dried figs and embrace them often. Roxanne speaks to me.

As we descend the sandstone, with no real path to follow, I notice by the way the horses tread how painful their feet must feel. During these 3500 kilometres, they have gone through all sorts of terrain without being properly shoed, proving how solid their hooves are. But I'm now so relieved to have shod their front feet. The descent from the peaks takes us about ten hours. Navigation is painful, the terrain is stony, and Roxanne is the one who knows the best way to go. We've gone through 30 agonising kilometres in the day. Before reaching Ride Out Cattle Station, where the owners, a couple and their daughter, are expecting us, I notice that my three companions are on the verge of sustaining wounds to their withers; things aren't happening according to plan. This grounds us for four days' rest, and I'm starting to feel that, before summer, taking a break will be unavoidable. I will not be able to do the entire Trail in one go. There, at the station, the family that welcomed us tell me that their grandfather covered part of the Trail at a time when it was still used by posties on horseback, in 1978 – that was *yesterday*. Their daughter plays the piano marvellously. I suddenly miss my family and feel quite lonely; it's often when I am with other people that I'm reminded of how solitary I am.

On the 12th of August, I'm in a forest and I stumble upon a solitary boar hunter. His trademark is to hunt with ferocious dogs without a gun. He takes on the feral pigs bare-handed, ties them up, takes photos … and then releases them. In order to partake in this out-of-the-ordinary sport, this Australian, in his forties, has made himself a camp with a fire pit, circled by stones, where he returns on a regular basis. He likes being there alone, bivouacking in the moonlight, practising this weaponless hunting method with his two faithful pig-hunting dogs. This exercise is as dangerous for the dogs as for their master. He invites me at nightfall to follow him. Brave but not foolhardy, I'm ready to climb the first tree if need be. I've been used to hunting in France with my father – I know that a boar is an intelligent, potentially very aggressive animal when she feels threatened. But everything goes well on this occasion, and I witness an original, no-kill form of hunting, stunned by his expertise.

My team and I travel a few days on the Calliope Range, west of Gladstone, the large east-coast port, and we move towards Calliope River for our appointment with the farrier.

Where I camp still isn't far from Mitch's home; taking advantage of this, he meets me with supplies for my steeds and for me. With Mitch, we get on – he knows exactly how to behave with horses. He's a real bushman. He's done a lot of mustering on big stations up north, chasing wild cattle. When I see him in the saddle for the first time, I realise he's as comfortable on horseback as on his tractor, and I start wondering if I couldn't make this trek with him. What attracts me most is that he appears to appreciate my freedom. Only, a voice tells me that I started my adventure alone and that I need to finish it alone. Mitch often tells me, 'You're the boss, you tell me.' He respects and admires the way I organise my crew. With each meeting I get to know him a little better. He's reserved and slightly unfathomable. But I do get his charm.

I've now been gone nine months. I've not much tasted the pleasures and comforts of civilisation during all this time and, perhaps because of it, they appear more and more attractive. It's hard to return to my nomadic life in the bush. When I'm weary, I think of all those who support me – those five thousand people I don't know from Adam who follow us on social media, and who send me encouraging messages, assuring me that our adventure is their dream. This fires me up.

My horses are also starting to show their lack of enthusiasm. They've acquired a tendency to loiter, even when I try enticing them with peanuts. Though the Trail isn't so exacting in Queensland, we still have many challenges to face – steep, narrow, rocky paths, where I have to place Roxanne, River and Cooper in single file. Cooper annoys me: he's the only one who demands to stop to release his droppings. On difficult tracks, whenever he halts, and since he walks in the middle of the group, he tugs on the horse in front and hinders the one behind. My troika is definitely portraying signs of weariness.

Around us, there are more palm trees, and bottle trees, which I particularly enjoy. I like the shape of the bottle tree, embodying its own name, its trunk like a large pitcher, which can reach up to 3.5 metres in diameter. We're travelling towards Rockhampton, a large town of eighty thousand inhabitants, which we skirt around towards the west.

The trail snakes its way through the Great Divide, but travelling north sometimes forces us to head south so as to navigate through the mountains – it drives me insane.

We zigzag towards the mountains. On Capricorn Highway, following the Tropic of Cancer from east to west, a camp is planned between the train track and the freeway. All this seems, to me, to be much too noisy and dangerous. Gigantic convoys of more than a hundred wagons filled with coal – I've counted them – relentlessly plough down the tracks. So, we duck under a railway bridge onto a path, overgrown with high grasses. I leave my team for a few minutes while I look for a safe spot. At that precise moment, a train thunders by, making the ground shake. My horses take fright, leap up the embankment and shoot off at full gallop straight towards the freeway. I stand frozen for a second, and then make a desperate attempt: I yell out my rallying call. To my absolute relief, they stop dead in their tracks. My heart is still galloping after my friends, adrenalin firing through my body. As soon as I catch up with them, we set off again – there is no way I'm staying here a second longer than necessary. I realise, in the aftermath, that they panicked because I wasn't with them.

We arrive in Kabra, a rural locality in the Rockhampton region on the verge of becoming a ghost town. It marks the end of Section 4 of the Trail. It's important for me to pause to appreciate these georgaphical landmarks, and to appreciate just how far I've come. I want to be able to know for sure that I've travelled the length and breadth of the BNT making no omissions whatsoever. After each leg, I reconnect with my fellow human beings at the pub, if there is one. And I do so again here. The locals offer me a paddock for my horses and a room for me. Both are welcome, and I'm so grateful to the town folk that night. My endeavour feels endless; weariness and a sense of routine has taken hold. Yet, something in me needs to push on.

11

A Much-Needed Break

Section 3: Kabra to Nebo

276 kilometres

1 September to 25 September 2016

At the foot of the Great Divide, the third-largest mountain range in the world, covering over 3500 kilometres along the Australian east coast, the landscape is burnt; according to the locals, the creeks and rivers could soon be dry. Water is rare around here and the land is parched. I meet the brother of a friend who lives nearby and who offers to help me find water. He's worked for seventeen years in the electrical power plant, a job that, he tells me, is monotonous. He lives alone with his dog. Even though he assures me that helping me on my expedition is a break for him, his kindness is exceptional.

We're riding towards Fitzroy River, where, for the first

time, I see a sign spelling out: 'Warning – Crocodiles!' I increase my vigilance. The locals here have given me the elementary precautions to take: no more bivouacs near a river, water the horses in different places each time and, above all, no deep waters. When I can see the riverbed through clear waters and if the flow is fast, I wash myself; if not, I use a bucket. Grass is scarce. I speak with the locals about the bushy terrain and the ravines, which slow down my progress, and they tell me about an unmarked shortcut. This helps me gain three hours. Roxanne, River and Cooper disappear up to their ears in the bushes, mostly lantana, with its orange flowers – such a prickly weed. Without landmarks, I have to use my compass. I see a lot of wildlife, including a wild sow with her piglets, who run away from us.

I am heading towards the Fitzroy River causeway to cross it safely. To avoid a huge detour, I decide to take a shortcut and bush-bash my way through bramble scrub and steep gullies. Wild boars, and emus, the second largest bird in the world, bolt in front of us, frightening my companions. The whole day is stressful, spent in hostile vegetation. It's very hot, and I'm relieved when I'm back on the track and find the crossing, thanks to a concrete bridge, as numerous signs continue to warn me of the presence of crocodiles lying in wait in this landscape of dense, bristly thickets.

Two days later, we arrive in the locality of Marlborough, where I have a talk with Craig and Shirley, who completed the Trail half on horseback, half in an incredible self-made caravan cart, which they offer to me to sleep in. A deep solidarity connects those who've lived through the Trail, having shared similar experiences.

It's the 7th of September. Mitch gives me a call and asks me if I can find a secure paddock for my horses. Earlier, I had told Mitch how much I missed the sea, after now ten months of adventure. My words hadn't fallen on deaf ears. A little later in the day, I watch as he arrives in a helicopter, with the objective of taking me to Stanage Bay and the islands beyond. I am really touched by this. He managed to convince his boss to lend him a chopper for a couple of days. He pilots gently, and proposes a stop so I can get some fresh air. It's a windy day and the flight is choppy. I feel slightly airsick. After an hour's flight above sea and vast swampy areas, a real bird sanctuary where innumerable ibis, egrets, ducks, and black swans congregate, as well as kangaroos and wild boars, we land right near the beach, opposite a pub. Then we visit wild Quail Island, a deserted paradise with turquoise waters and waves crashing on rock faces. I perk up … We swim naked in the waves, and spend two days together before he brings me back. His charm and calm temperament are strangely compelling. We leave in his bright-blue helicopter, a Robinson R22, often used for mustering – as Mitch has done for years up north on huge cattle stations. The larrikin helicopter zigzags agilely between the trees, above the kangaroos – now that my stomach can deal with it. It is a stunning getaway, and this man displays treasure-like qualities that draw me to him – but nothing will stop me from finishing the Trail alone with my brumbies, even if my feelings for Mitch have been growing.

I must admit that it's been getting harder and harder to return to the bush. The Trail seems to have no end. I'm riding towards a deserted location, once a mining town, where a few pensioners remain, living in corrugated-iron shacks. The pub, which was transported here on wheels, drawn by a team of oxen, isn't in business anymore; the place is too down at heel. I camp very close to what's left of it, before following the Bruce Highway for 20 kilometres. I hate these sections along motorways. They're dangerous; the cars speed by like bullets. In a rest area, the coffee is free – this is to encourage drivers to take a break because of the interminable distances. Many people use the opportunity to also come to see us and ask questions. I explain about my trek, and tell them about my horses, captured in the wild and patiently trained.

This section I'm in seems particularly endless. It runs through cattle stations, and my brumbies hardly have enough grass to eat. On the 17th of September, on the way to Nebo – a township of 443 inhabitants, north-west of Brisbane – I decide to temporarily stop following the Trail in a week. We've covered 4000 kilometres in ten months. Heavy-hearted in the terrible heat, I don't have a penny to my name and my companions still display signs of sores on their withers, even if their health seems excellent otherwise. I come around to accepting that I can't fight nature, the exhausting heat, the chaotic weather – rains, tropical storms, cyclones – and the lack of money. It's all too much. But I'm not giving up. I'm just taking a break. I thank all those on social media, in such numbers, who have fed, helped, cared for, advised and supported us. Returning to reality, returning to work, earning money will demand an enormous effort from me. Apart from the sadness, a feeling of failure dogs me, that I've waited too long. I haven't known when to stop this long trek.

The decision now made, I want to take advantage, in spite of my exhaustion, of this last week in the expanse of bush with my four-legged family. But my inner engine has stalled. Mentally, I feel I'll never get to the end of this week. Everything seems overwhelming. To add insult to injury, the sky turns against me, too, bringing us only rain. I scrape through the miserable days – I'm saturated. I follow the road, feeling alone, dragging my boots, which have also started giving up the ghost, after swallowing so many stones. It rains and rains, and I feel just about ready to curl up into a ball under a tree until someone comes to get me. A humid, tropical heat crushes us. My horses are struggling, their heads dripping with sweat. Every afternoon, new storms surprise us. We hobble on, now back on the mountain tops, still five days from Nebo. I make camp, a fire, and a shelter out of a nylon tarp on four posts. I put a few branches under it; when it rains, I'll know where to find dry wood.

Just when everything seems lost, an encounter changes everything. As I ride through an enormous cattle station, called Marylands, I meet a wonderful family, a couple and their children, who offer me a day's rest in their home. They have a physically disabled son, who can hardly speak and moves with difficulty. This family offers me a singular, unexpected light. The mother, Leoni, taught her son Kodia everything – to read, to write – without ever being able to send him to school. He takes part in all the work on the farm with his parents and brothers and sisters. He's happy, and even rides on horses. This young man impresses me so much. I marvel at the way he manages himself. We connect immediately and a special bond forms between us.

I bless the Trail for bringing me to meet such generous people. We spend a day mustering together, branding the cattle, dehorning and castrating calves. I love this work, in contact with the animals, which, in this part of the country, is done out in the open air from one end of the year to the other. I learn a lot about cattle work during this visit.

After leaving them, miserable at the idea of arriving in Nebo on my own and overwhelmed by a feeling of non-achievement for interrupting my trek before the end, I contact my childhood friend Emilie. We were in the same class at school in France and, by pure fluke, she now lives in Sydney. I beg her to come to help me celebrate the 4000 kilometres my horses and I have left behind us. I want to mark the occasion.

It's raining again, and I feel brain dead. Each day, the challenge is greater. Mozzies assault us in tight brigades; my horses must feel my despair. Roxanne starts playing tricks on me, and escapes from time to time. My day's rest had been taken up with branding cattle. I've got hay fever, and I'm starving. I'd really like someone to come to get me. I think of Mitch, but he's far away and I know it's not going to happen. However, I must set up camp. Near a river this time. The water is clean, and we are too far inland to worry about the danger of crocodiles. I don't have any telephone connection. I add some more duct tape around my boots to keep their soles attached to their body. Even Fox, usually so full of life, is KO.

When the sun reappears, my exhaustion vanishes, and I resurface. The strength to be happy in the bush with my dear friends returns. I stop feeling sorry for myself and allow myself to appreciate the beautiful moments. I pick up feathers, which I love, and put them on my hat. As soon as I can, I take a swim. After so many ups and downs, the sun and the prospect of seeing my friend Emilie – the idea of celebrating with her – and, if all goes smoothly, getting some phone connection, settle me. I'm two days from Nebo.

Like the faithful friend she is, Emilie hops on a plane, rents a car and comes to see me in this improbable location, bringing invaluable cheeses, champagne and a baguette. Will she ever realise how grateful I am? Thank you, Emilie. During these two days with my childhood mate, we drink to our reunion, to the thousands of kilometres travelled thanks to my heroic brumbies, to the joy of being together, to dancing in the bush. Happiness. In a large waterhole surrounded by bushes, safe from all danger, I swim, and bathe on Cooper's back. The presence of Emilie, who's on River's back, is a true comfort, and I feel as though a magic wand of reassurance has been waved over us.

I've chosen to interrupt the Trail in Nebo because this locality is a hundred kilometres from Mackay on the east coast, which is close to the start of Section 3, the section I'm abandoning for the time being. We trot on an asphalted road, excited by our promised break. I howl like a dingo and stop for a photograph in front of the sign indicating Nebo. The calendar says it's the 25th of September 2016; ten months and eight days, or 313 days, have gone by since we set off.

With my companions, we parade up the main street, in front of the town hall. I'm riding Roxanne. She's confident and can feel my relief. We stop in front of the pub – a lovely old building, which is a reminder of the settlers' era of glory; spitting image of a Western. Nebo Hotel gives me a room for half the price. Roxanne, Cooper and River are going to enjoy the rodeo ground. I thank them, pat them, feed them and take care of them. I'm resolute about finishing the Trail in the following months. But in the pub, Emilie and I celebrate my interrupted ordeal, along with the miners and the locals. Fox is part of the festivities, and he shares my steak and French fries.

A group of kids on their school holiday are camping on the rodeo ground for a pony-club weekend. The facilitator asks me to give a talk about my trek, and all the planning it involved beforehand. I accept happily. Emilie returns to Sydney, and my truck-driver friend Kris, who helped me transport my horses south at the start of the trek, has come back to pick us up and take us back to Dorrigo. A beautiful, familiar pasture awaits my mates, where they can spend the summer months in a cooler temperature.

On the road back to square one, I experience the odd sensation of taking just three days to return along the hundreds and hundreds of kilometres that were so many painful months to accomplish on the way up. We take advantage of the opportunity to stop in Byron Bay to introduce my brumbies to the sea that I so cherish. I invite some good friends to meet us on the beach – I want them to meet my heroes and to share a picnic. I take Roxanne, River and Cooper, one after the other, to taste the salty water and feel it on their skin; the sea has healing benefits for horses' legs. Apart from the iodised air, the salt water temporarily relieves their joints and tendons of some of their weight, and helps them cool off. After their bath, my companions roll in the sand, to dry themselves and get rid of the salt. They deserve this treat.

In Dorrigo, I find Erica. I leave my three friends to their holiday. They'll put some weight back on while I'm away, grazing in a beautiful pasture, and I know they'll be happy.

12

'Alenor, Alenor!' Yell the Children

Return to Pukatja desert
30 October 2016 to 20 March 2017

I'm on my way back to the desert. I'm returning to work in Pukatja, an Aboriginal community located 200 kilometres south-east of Uluru. I know this place well, because this is where I worked for a year before starting the Trail.

Employed by the Ngaanyatjarra Pitjantjatjara Yankunytjatjara Women's Council, my task is to keep some ninety kids busy from the time they come out of school at the start of the afternoon until the evening, as well as during weekends, with their families' support. This organisation, which was created in the eighties by a group of Indigenous women, originally to fight against domestic abuse, has extended its action exponentially to include nutrition and other help for elders, and to include support for pregnant women, and children.

The teenagers and the young kids of the community know me already and cry out my name, '*Alenor, Alenor!*', as soon as I step outside my door. I organise sporting, recreational, artistic and educational activities. My job is varied. The children are often talented in music and painting. I organise workshops, and prepare meals, keen to show them how to eat healthily. Without these activities, mostly left to their own devices, they often find themselves at risk of engaging in dangerous behaviour; substance abuse, vandalism and theft are always a threat. The community counts some four hundred people, though this number fluctuates: many of the inhabitants are itinerant, and move around a lot; parents go to see their families; others are in prison or go to Alice Springs, and their absence prolongs itself. Many of the children suffer from real social issues. My role is to be a link between the families, the school and the social services, to try to iron out difficulties.

The guidance of the community elders is invaluable. We regularly visit sacred places, and we go hunting for honey ants, or searching for witchetty grubs or goannas. In the service four-wheel drive, allotted to me with the job, we take off for picnics, and sit under the gigantic acacias, near dry riverbeds, eating grilled kangaroo tails. I take young kids to camp out under the moon, to swim in the desert rockholes. They love these happy times – and I do, too. There's such beauty in the desert; one has to enjoy it.

For ten years now, I've worked in twenty-odd communities in Australia's Red Centre, many of which I've returned to multiple times, in the same capacity, nurturing my bond with the children and the families. They have shared many secrets of their culture with me and have taught me to feel comfortable in their environment. They've instilled in me a little of their intimate relationship with the natural elements, and have taught me to be self-sufficient, to always find resources in the wilderness. Walking in the bush with the Aboriginal children, I've learnt to find my bearings, thanks to a broken branch or yellow grasses, and to get to the place I need to reach. I consider it a privilege to have experienced their traditions – not in books but in the field, among those who have accepted me.

But my work is also emotionally draining. After months on the Trail, the return to Pukatja demands mountains of energy and determination. When looking after so many children on your own, you can't relax your attention for a second. Isolation, the desert, the crushing heat, the abandoned dogs (I've got five at my place, along with a few donkeys who come to drink) – all this constitutes my everyday environment. Two policemen, five teachers, two nurses and the two staff from the small supermarket are, apart from myself, the only non-Indigenous people in Pukatja. I've always been haunted by the savage immensity of this isolated place, the palettes of greens, from the spinifex and the shrubs, to the gums, with their piercing white trunks rising from the red dirt; from the big, sandy riverbeds and the waterholes, with their granite boulders, to the ranges in the distance. I'm moved by these children, growing freely as part of several extended families. More often than not, the grandmothers are the ones to bring the children up. The babes, with their beautiful large brown eyes and straw-coloured hair, carried on the hips of the little girls, have eternally leaky noses and live half-naked. The teenagers choose to have violet or green hair, and, curious of everything, imitate the pictures in the fashion magazines.

The two months of school holidays makes my stay in Pukatja problematic. The absence of school and of social services during the period adds to my burden. The building that was devoted to extracurricular activities has burnt down. Left to their own devices, the children often come and knock on my door, to eat a piece of fruit or look at my computer. The days are long, and I have few tools at my disposal. I'm alone, and mustn't let myself get overwhelmed – which is easier said than done. For more efficiency and a little bit more discipline, activities are organised according to the days of the week. The community is spread out, and families don't have cars; I must go and pick up the kids in the four-wheel drive, make circuits, bring home those who live further away, urge on the uncooperative ones or those who are a little sick, keep an eye on the children who have been taken in by other families, and on the very young ones who can't yet walk. I'm on the go all the time.

I establish a day for sport – basketball, in this instance – and a day for lunch, which I prepare with plenty of proteins, like minced meat, using a vacated hall for the purpose. Other days are devoted to music, with instruments made available for teenagers keen to make their own tunes. One afternoon is devoted to make-up and hairdressing, and there is also a computer-skills course. Another class concentrates on multimedia – making videos, recording music and taking photos are the kids' absolute favourite. An evening of ear-splitting dancing is organised for the teenagers, who are often accompanied by a parent or younger brothers and sisters, who are just as good at wriggling their hips as their elders. I bring the sound system, and the disco is on. The girls dance among themselves, as do the boys – and not at the same time. Their modesty is extreme; I must be careful not to offend them. These activities generally end rather late and, being responsible for each child, I take a number of them back home.

Not a day goes by without the need to resolve a family issue. Whether it be to drive, sometimes quite far, a young woman wanting to return to her home; to take a youngster to the local dispensary; to provide food for a mother suddenly finding herself temporarily destitute; or to visit a wife facing domestic abuse – all these jobs are part of my duties. I must be a super nanny, a taxi driver, a chief scout, a storyteller, a school assistant, an older sister. I patch up minor ailments. I listen to grievances.

My main source of pride is when I am sometimes able to convince a teenager, whose studies appeal to them, to go to boarding school to attend college – with the family's agreement, of course. The challenge is then for them to accept staying there as a border, far from their families and removed from their culture.

Every morning, I report the last day's events, as well as the costs incurred, to my supervisors, who work in offices hundreds of kilometres away. I convey the details of the problems at hand or attempt to get the green-light for a specific need. Far from everything, my mobile phone is the best way to keep up with my family and friends. Pukatja is one of the rare communities, and was the first, to have mobile service. Mitch calls me often. He's attentive to the narrative of my days. We exchange texts daily, swapping favourite songs; I follow his advice. Imperceptibly, the feeling that we're weaving a strong bond becomes more and more obvious to me.

When I have a break, I go to Uluru to renew myself. There, after a few hours' drive on a red track – when violent storms don't block the road – I can meet friends and drink beer; in the community where I work, alcohol is forbidden because of the ravages it has caused. At one point, the people from the production company who came to film me on the Trail turn up at Pukatja, to take images of wild horses in a desert environment.

I have invested so much of myself and have become so fond of the children during this interval that, when the time comes to leave them, I feel as if I am abandoning them. But the five months without seeing Roxanne, River and Cooper have been tough. I miss my companions – and the Trail is calling me again. I haven't finished with it. I invest my salary in resuming the expedition I assigned myself – even if I sometimes flirt with the idea of staying here in Pukatja. But this would result in too much unfinished business, and the thought crosses my mind for only an instant.

13
Return to the Trail after Cyclone Debbie

End of Section 3: Nebo to Collinsville

300 kilometres

14 April to 22 April 2017

My decision is made. I board an airliner to meet my horses in Dorrigo, and from there we return to Nebo in a truck, where I can get back into the saddle. The break has been beneficial: we've got our strength back and especially our enthusiasm. On the 28th of March 2017, as we approach Brisbane, the most murderous cyclone in forty years – Cyclone Debbie, resulting in fourteen deaths – hits Queensland, taking us hostage. Bridges are destroyed, houses are underwater, thousands of inhabitants are evacuated, and the corpses of cattle float on waterways clogged with the trunks of fallen trees and every kind of debris. A thousand kilometres of coastline has been damaged. There's nothing to do but wait for the roads to be cleared. Torrential rain falls in Nebo – a metre per day. The Trail hasn't escaped the disaster, and it's only on the 14th of April that I'm officially allowed to travel, with Roxanne, Cooper and River in fine fettle. The weather is radiant, but there seems to be so much water.

On a high, I'm impatient to return to the unknown, to the rhythm of my brumbies' step, and to pure, unadulterated nature. I'm mad enough to believe that in two and a half months we'll have reached the end. For the time being, the geography is very flat, without much notable challenge. We're ten days away from finishing Section 3. My horses haven't forgotten their good habits. The countryside is green and thick with grass. The time is ripe for travel. It's not so hot and, in principle, the rain season is over. I sleep one night at Exmoor Station, a large farm. The family has offered me their staff premises. Their four-year-old daughter, Jezebel, rides bareback on River, who stays calm and gentle – a total angel.

I manage to cross Bowen River, which is infested with crocodiles, on a concrete passageway; I don't dillydally. I follow up with another farm, where the owners' five young children bewitch me. They're so relaxed, free, and cooperative, already helping their parents with all sorts of jobs. They're all horse-mad and show off their riding skills in the round yard on their station horses. I inspect Bowen River, still overflowing and clogged with tree trunks – we can't avoid taking detours on the roads. Cyclone Debbie was so violent that some of the trees still standing hold other uprooted trees in their branches, witnesses of the rising water and furious winds. Fox, who's getting older, suffers from arthritis because of the humidity; I carry him or put him on my saddle.

It takes me a week to get to Collinsville, a cattle-breeding, coal-mining town, 1245 kilometres from Brisbane and about 50 kilometres from the sea. My first stop is to visit school children, all of them in their bright-blue uniforms.

I take my companions to a rodeo ground, which hasn't much to offer: no shower, no toilet, not even a shelter. It's raining again, and I catch sight of a hotel, where I learn that a room has been reserved for me and paid for. This amount of thoughtfulness can only have come from Mitch. I take a day's rest, and the next morning, there he is – he's turned up by surprise, after hopping in a plane and renting a car. Through all those days of hard work and effort in Pukatja, Mitch was always present, with his messages and phone calls. His support is precious. I'm so touched by his constancy and encouragements.

I manage to take Fox to the vet in Mackay on the coast, so he can get intramuscular injections to relieve his arthritis. Fox is my best friend, my brother, my companion, my confidant. The few legs of the way I had to make without his presence were much harder. I'm never alone when he's there beside me. He shares my tent, and at night, by the fire, I massage his stiff legs and take all the burrs out of his soft, long fur.

14

Conquer or Perish

Section 2: Collinsville to Mount Misery

560 kilometres

22 April to 10 June 2017

One thing is particularly bothering me: Burdekin Falls, on the eponymous river – an enormous, 876-metre-long and 37-metre-high dam, built for irrigation purposes, about a week away from Collinsville. Because of the cyclone and the floods, I learn that it's impassable for the time being. The road has been opened, but the dam wall hasn't, and I can't wait at the foot of the dam, running the risk of food being lacking for my companions, as well as for myself. It's still very hot – 33 to 35 degrees Celsius – and Fox is not in good shape, unlike Roxanne, Cooper and River. A heaven-sent woman houses us for a few days, until the dam reopens and we're free to go.

189

It will take us another five days to reach the dam wall. On the way, in front of another property gate, we're welcomed by cows who seem to have been waiting for us peacefully. They're white Brahmans, a breed imported from India in the past, who can withstand arid climates. In getting in or out of a station, I'm sometimes faced with a nightmare: it's necessary to use pliers to open up fences and then to put them back together again – a very slow and demanding task. In these rural areas, cattle are often curious, and two hundred cows can follow you away from their owner's land at any given time.

We cross Bowen River, populated with crocodiles, and I notice all the damage. The road straddling it has just been freed of the sand shifted by Cyclone Debbie.

I arrive at one of the oldest pubs in Australia – a heritage-listed, 1865 wooden structure, built by the pionneers of this cattle and sheep-breeding station. The original bark roof was replaced with corrugated iron, but the inner decoration is a testimony of the building's history. Old paintings, Chippendale chairs, trophies, tools, horseshoes and a photograph of Slim Dusty, as well as photographs of the rodeo ground, crowd the old walls, which have seen so much. A stuffed crocodile hangs from a beam – a very local trophy.

I set my horses free in a paddock abutting the pub, where I have a drink with the locals. I chat with Earl, a charming man of seventy-five years of age, with a well-rounded Aussie middle, blue-eyes and an affable smile. Christian, a helicopter pilot, joins us for dinner. I gather information from him about the condition of the country ahead and what to expect. He proposes to take me the next day on a reconnaissance flight – a proposal I cannot refuse. Earl belongs to the rodeo committee, and, as such and in spite of his pacemaker, is making repairs to the rodeo yards on his own. I give him a hand during the day. Bush people are hard workers.

Grass is scarce. I drop bags of pellets for my brumbies during the flight with Christian. The next day, my three companions are rolling around in the mud of a small dam, after a sweaty day. They're happy that I have pellets for them.

The logistics of this gigantic state are complex. I ride through many farms, which I'm supposed to warn of my arrival, but, truth be told, there's hardly ever any mobile network; in general, the owners are warned of my presence by the bush telegraph. In this area, the Trail is barely marked. Land surveys are obsolete, and updates need to be printed. Detecting a landmark looking vaguely like a Trail sign isn't an obvious pursuit.

During the expedition, I've become a real pro at packing gear. Before leaving on the 14th of April, I lightened the load, attempting to constrain myself to the bare minimum.

However, the morning ritual is still respected, and preparing to get back on the road after each bivouac isn't any faster.

Cyclone Debbie has generated clouds of mozzies, and for a few days I've been feeling very, very tired. I push on, telling myself I'm getting soft. Everywhere, the water is disgusting, with dead cows lying on the edge of the dams. They're my only source of drinking water, once the water is filtered – the operation is long and fiddly and a real drag. It consists of letting the water drip through a cloth pouch hooked to a tree, then pouring it through another filter, three or four times – depending on the state of the water – before boiling it.

On the 1st of May, two days from reaching Burdekin Falls, we reach an impressive dam named Dalrymple Lake, well known for its barramundi fishing. The Trail forces me to move south, which messes with my bearings. I haven't managed to get my mind around travelling south with the sun's path going in the opposite direction, and I set up my camp facing it. I'm now seriously sunburnt. My whole body hurts and my muscles are painful. It's a meltdown. I imagine this to be the result of my months-long break. I'm not as fit as I was, and my muscles must have lost their elasticity.

The cyclone has weakened a lot of trees. I have to choose a camp location with great care if I don't want us to end up crushed under a branch. While I have my dinner, Roxanne and River position their heads above me, like two beggars, wanting to share my pittance. Roxanne warms her belly by the fire. In the morning, the light is out of this world, but Cooper hasn't got shoes on his back feet and they're hurting him. I have only shod their front feet as 70 per cent of a horse's weight is on the forelegs. As soon as I've taken care of my friends, I'm always desperate to down a can of sardines. I take care to sweep my 'ephemeral home' and put everything away, to keep up my morale. The constant pain, as well as the spectacle of all the corpses of cows lying around dams, is depressing.

At night, I sometimes wake up with a start, having lost all my bearings. I'm seized with terror, thinking myself alone on Earth. Then I grab Fox, hear my brumbies' bells, and realise where I am. Panic dispels – I'm not alone. I go back to sleep. Feverish, I refuse to admit to myself that something is wrong. My joints are hurting horribly. I attribute these aches and pains to not being fit enough. Rashes have also begun to appear on my legs.

This morning, a big day is ahead of me, with the prospect of crossing Burdekin Falls. The dirt track leading to it takes hours. Finally, I catch sight of the falls in the distance. It's nine in the morning – fishermen offer me a beer. *Why not!* This eight-hour journey has no end. We're at the foot of the dam at last and, against all expectations, I'm eager to carry on. We're stopped by a strange contraption on this track, a temporary red light in the middle of nowhere. The light changes to green and we step onto the passageway, deafened by the blasting pandemonium of the waterfall. My horses take fright, Cooper the most anxious. I guide them and reassure them by walking in front of them, dominating the roar. The extent of the construction work and the power of the water are astounding. Cormorants dry their wings on the flat rocks on the other side of the barrage. The water level comes up flush with the top of the dam. A few days earlier, crossing the passageway was prohibited. On top of the hill where the fishermen are camping, there's no mobile network and no shelter. I'm disappointed and spent. I release the horses and fall in a heap. I'm going to meet the dam manager to whom I have had some food rations sent. I attempt to organise feed for my brumbies, as there's very little grass. Skilled drillers are on site – we're three hours from Townsville, and one of them kindly brings me some feed for my horses. Dead-beat, I lie down. For a week now, I've been plagued with high nocturnal fevers, tremors and strange sweats.

It's the next morning, and I've organised a day for rest. I wake up wracked with pain. I don't get up as early as usual, and I can hardly crawl out of my tent. My stomach and legs are covered with red blotches. It's the 3rd of May – we've only been back on the road for three weeks. Putting on my boots involves a considerable effort, and makes me want to sob. Something isn't right. I gather all my strength to climb to the top of the hill, hoping to get some mobile service so I'll be able to call Erica. The line is bad, the conversation choppy; I explain my paralysing symptoms. Erica, concerned, thinks it's a tropical fever – Ross River fever. She advises me to get to a populated area for treatment – but there's no enclosure to leave the horses in. A young woman, Layne Pritchard, comes to mind. She had offered to provide help if I were in need of it. She lives on a station near here. I get hold of her and tell her my problem. She points out where her farm is: a three-hour ride. I gather all my remaining strength, and stuff myself with anti-inflammatories and painkillers. I saddle Roxanne, my indefectible rock, and my three brumbies and I set off towards the station.

In the hilly landscape, we leave the road and ride through the paddocks in the direction that she gave me. When we get there, a helicopter is mustering cattle. Someone is riding up on a motorbike just as I arrive at the house. The helicopter lands, and the pilot, Layne's father, Wayne Pritchard, welcomes me. I explain the situation. He offers me a paddock for my horses and asks the policeman in the closest village to come to pick me up to take me to the goldmine, to find out what the paramedics there can do to relieve me. I have to leave Fox at the farm.

The mine is an hour away. The nurses take my temperature and tell me I'm presenting all the symptoms of Ross River fever. It's a nasty one, creating havoc in one's system. Transmitted by mosquito bites, it wrecks the joints and, because there's no remedy for it, the symptoms are long lasting. I must go to the closest hospital, in Townsville. A mine worker drives me there. On the way, he proposes to put me up in the event I have to stay on the spot. He drops me at the emergency department and gives me his details. A blood test confirms the diagnosis: I test positive for Ross River fever. I'm in despair. They don't have anything much to give me, apart from a few analgesics and some stronger anti-inflammatories than those in my kit. I'm told that I'll be down for the count for at least three months and there's no way in hell I'll be able to finish my trek.

Endemic to Australia and Papua New Guinea, the virus infects an average of more than five thousand people a year. An arbovirus, it was first isolated in 1959 from Ross River mosquitoes, precisely near Townville. In short, this virus is no joke.

After going through so many obstacles – facing snow, torrential rain, scorching heat, and chewing up literally thousands of kilometres – how could this idiotic, microscopic beast defeat me so close to my goal? I'm shattered at the idea of abandoning my dream so close to the end. Other people who've been subjected to this virus on the Trail have had to give up. I can think of only one thing: returning to my journey, being reunited with my horses and with Fox. This illness is not going to stop me. I give myself a week to see if the meds will alleviate the pain – and then I'll know if I'm capable of taking to the road again.

Because of the swarms of innumerable mosquitoes, tics and insects of all kinds, Layne, twenty years of age with a beautiful cowboy hat on her head, and her father, Wayne, have advised me to hang an insecticide cattle eartag around my horses' necks to deter some of the relentless buffalo flies, horse flies and mosquitoes. Horses can catch Ross River fever, too. I wash their backs with Betadine to avoid infection from irritation brought on by the heat and insects.

In vain, I try to contact Mitch several times. He's detained in a remote place, and so, on his voicemail, I leave the phone number for Old Glenroy Station, where Wayne Pritchard and his daughters have generously put me up until I get better. Everyone is extremely understanding, helpful and truly kind. Bush solidarity is something to behold.

Mitch calls me at last. The fever has dropped very slightly, but the nigh-unbearable joint pain remains. He proposes to meet me at Ravenswood, a little village four days away from where I'm staying. I need to know if I have the strength to carry on and also if he is able to help me. The rashes on my legs have abated slightly. I'm naive enough to think that all will be improved within a week. I set off, in spite of being totally exhausted. In camp, with my horses, I sometimes lie down under a tree while they lick the soles of my feet. Every one of my muscles is in agony. 'Cooper, will you please put up my tent for me?' My whole body is off on a trek of its own, leaving me behind with the pain. I have a feeling that my companions understand what's going on.

Four days later, we arrive, as anticipated, in Ravenswood, known for its goldmine. Mitch will get there on the 18th of May. This keeps me going. People here are friendly and ready to oblige; they're used to helping each other out. In the old pub, with its quaint charm, I'm expected, with Lucerne hay waiting for my team. I drink with the locals. One of them is a wheelchair-bound Anzac veteran, who commemorates the Australian soldiers who fell fighting with the Allies every 25th of April. This is such a balm after the past few days, which have nearly done me in and sapped all my energy.

Mitch spoils me. Driving thirty hours to rush to my rescue doesn't bother him. The care he takes goes to my heart, even the simplest thing like bringing me a clean shirt, some chocolate, a book – *The Mountain Shadow* by Gregory David Roberts. I'd liked his *Shantaram*, the Australian enfant terrible's earlier bestseller. I'm sometimes nearly embarrassed by Mitch's tender thoughtfulness – does one ever feel deserving of that kind of care? He declares he's got two weeks to dedicate to me: he lightens my load with his presence and his help. This fills me with a new breath of life. Earl, the older gentleman from the rodeo ground near the old bush pub, has lent him a four-wheel drive ute to use as a support vehicle. I leave Ravenswood with Roxanne, River and Cooper. Mitch, transporting my equipment and the pack saddle, goes ahead to assess the terrain, looking for watering places and good camp locations that have feed for my horses. Fox gets to ride in the car with Mitch and save his tired legs.

I'm demanding a lot of my body by riding six or eight hours a day. To overcome the pain, I take high doses of medication, setting the alarm on my phone for 4am so I can take some more, and be fit before daybreak. My wrists and hands hurt so much that I can't even get the pills out of their box. I'm nearly in tears, and so thankful for Mitch's help. Cyclone Debbie has gone, but we still have to deal with strong rains. A sudden flood forces us to halt for three days, staying in Mingela's pub. The total count of Mingela's population is two: the owners of the pub.

We carry on our journey. My horses have to swim across the rivers in flood. I have water up to my chest and the current is strong. I get my brumbies around the grid bridges one at a time. They're in perfect symbiosis with me, and don't flinch. Yet, it's a daily ordeal. We prepare lovely bivouacs. Mitch assists me in every way. It's such a relief to follow this trek with a man who makes light of every difficulty. He's so comfortable in himself, so tranquil, so happy in the bush, that everything becomes a pleasure. He's the son and grandson of graziers on a vast station, where they've been breeding cattle for generations. On these isolated farms, you have to learn how to do everything and how to rely solely on yourself. It's a pure delight to share the toughness of nature, its sorrows and its joys. Without this human being, I don't know if I'd have been able to carry on.

The pain isn't going, but I'm learning to live with it. Cooper has lost a shoe and people we've met on the road guide us to their station, where we can camp and get Cooper re-shod. I discover the donkey heater: an enormous tin container heated on a wood fire and connected to a pipe, which delivers a hot shower. I administer Fox some more anti-inflammatory injections for his arthritis, which helps him out, and he spends time in the four-wheel drive with Mitch.

The rains have been so unforgiving that, in front of us, I see a bridge lying at the bottom of the stream, but the rivers become less dangerous as we progress. Now we're moving inland, I can swim with my brumbies. My joints are still painful when I get off the saddle. It's a deep hurt, throbbing and invasive. The croaking of frogs pervades the night and the day pulses with the song of birds. My companions are revelling in the good grass. The vegetation is thriving after all the torrential rains. Mitch stays with me until we reach the station owned by one of the Trail coordinators, Helen, who puts us up. Then, he has to go back to work. Despite the sadness of being separated, I'm determined to pursue the Trail. I know that we'll find each other again.

I organise the arrival of Cat Vinton, an English photographer I met briefly in London. Specialising in documenting expeditions, she is consumed by nomadic life around the world. Living among tribes, she documents their way of life to help preserve their unique culture. She travels on her own funds, and the logistics of rural Australia are not simple. My friend Earl has kindly offered to pick her up at the nearest airport on the coast, to house her for a night and to then drive her all the way to me. For this appointment, I've organised for us to meet at a station called Kangaroo Hill – a good-sounding name – where I arrive alone, two days before their arrival. It's a gigantic station, managed by Melissa. In spite of my total exhaustion, I do a day's mustering to thank my hostess. The mustering crew includes a helicopter, two young women, an older couple, the property owner and myself, all on horseback. We gather two thousand heads over kilometres, and yard them before spending the afternoon drafting them. As I gallop after some escaping cattle during this tough day in the dust, I lose my feather adorned hat, which has been with me all along the Trail. When I get back, a nearly tame emu terrifies my mounts, who gallop off in spite of their hobbles. By the end, we're all dead-beat.

The next day, the 1st of June, I'm impatient to see Cat. I'd planned for rations for the two of us to be sent to the farm. Earl and Cat have trouble locating us in this endless expanse of land. It's nice to see Earl again, and I'm grateful for his help. That night, we celebrate our reunion with several drinks. This is an opportunity to test the resilience of this hardy young woman, who must walk with 20 kilograms of equipment on her back. I've sent rations for the two of us on to stations ahead to lighten our load a little.

Cat is a good soldier; she manages to keep up with my horses' rhythm – a fast one: 7 kilometres per hour. We don't know each other well but we're on the same wavelength. She explains that she wants to observe the four of us for several days before starting to take photographs, in order to understand the essence of what she's trying to capture. She decides she wants to encapsulate the link that bonds my three companions and me. She's not very tall and her backpack looms over her head and descends to the top of her thighs. It's heavy, and I suggest that she give me some of her equipment to carry in order to lighten her load. During the day, it gets hot and she turns crimson, but she never complains. Unfortunately, I can't add her equipment to my packhorse, who's already at capacity, carrying all the camping equipment and the basic food rations for the two of us for the long period of isolation in the bush.

Luckily, both Cat's mental and physical strength are out of the ordinary: she resembles Roxanne in this. I suggest that she ride my horse, but she refuses, seeing how painful my joints are. In fact, I realise that I'm incapable of walking. We share the tent, and in the middle of the night she gives me the anti-inflammatories that will enable me to get up a few hours later. I try to conceal the pain I'm in and sometimes offer to take up her backpack, but I can't hoodwink her, and she very rarely accepts. Her spirit, her motivation, are a blessing. That someone like her chose to come with me has been an inspiration. Our connection is instant and needs no introduction. She melds into our family as if she has always belonged to it. After a few days' immersion, she's understood the essence of my adventure and begins capturing the unique quality of my relationship with my companions. The way she has intuited the spirit of our slow voyage – forging its way on, bit by bit, and never giving up – really touches me.

The hand she lends me with the daily tasks is also a precious help. She adapts to our rhythm and respects our rituals and behaviours. She adopts our way of life, and the horses appreciate her as she blends her footsteps with theirs. In short, we're a perfect team. We laugh a lot, saying we carry on like a couple of hardened bachelors – and our jokes make many a hurdle lighter.

The graziers in the area have warned us about the presence of poison bait, to cull the overpopulation of wild dogs, who constantly attack the cattle. I'm constrained to keeping Fox on a lead – Fox, who has never experienced such curtailment of his freedom. But it's stressful to have to keep an eye on him twenty-four hours a day.

Everything is becoming a succession of long red-dirt tracks following endless flat lands and endless, uninterrupted straight lines. Bloody Queensland, where one horizon chases the next – further and further away! We try to not lose our minds by playing riddles. We're moving towards a remote place, where very large cattle stations have been established. We hardly meet anyone. When we come across a farmer, I ask if he can drop Cat's backpack at our next camp to give her some relief.

This all-terrain photographer has chosen an extraordinary existence, which bestows total freedom upon her. Travelling to the four corners of the globe, she has lived with nomads in Mongolia; with the salt caravaners and their yaks in the Himalayas; with sea nomads in Burma, and in the Andaman Islands in India; with the Sámi people and their reindeers in Finland; as well as with Tibetans. Everywhere, she shares the lives of those she photographs. She knows how to adapt to every situation. On this endless trek, she's providing living proof of it. The temperature falls to 1 degree at night; the weather is not in our favour. But this morning the sky is clear, with azure blue bleeding into purple in its furthest reaches. After seeing the weather forecast, a day's rest seems to be a good idea, and I use this opportunity to pamper my brumbies, while Cat takes photos of the bivouac – she measures our harmony with nature. We're crossing a large station called

Gunnawarra, where the Atkinsons, the owners, house us in the seasonal workers' shed, which has a shower. Cat is offered a spin in a helicopter so she can take a few aerial shots. The epic of Section 2 ends on the 11th of June with the sound of rotor blades. We're close to our goal.

15
Thalassa! Thalassa![*]

Section 1: Mount Misery to Cooktown

458 kilometres

12 June to 20 July 2017

At the end of the road is the sea. I'm dreaming of a camp on the beach. On the 12th June, we enter the last section of the Trail, the one and only part to open out onto the Pacific Ocean. I'm amazed to be so close to the end. Cat and I have tapped deeply into our reserves of strength to end this journey before her return to Europe, which is fixed for the 5th of July.

Her presence is infinitely encouraging. I'm on my last legs, drugged up to the eyeballs on medication. I attempt to

---

[*] 'Thalassa! Thalassa!' ('The Sea! The Sea!') cried the ten thousand Greek mercenaries on their return from Persia, after an epic journey of 6000 kilometres through mountains and deserts, as related by their leader, Xenophon, a general, and a disciple of Socrates, in his book *Anabasis*.

conceal the pain, but the slightest wrong movement elicits a screech of agony. Cat is aware that, by the end of the day, my whole body is hurting and I can hardly move. After two days, we reach Innot Hot Springs in the Tablelands, a region of plateaus and waterfalls. As its name indicates, hot springs can be found around here. The Mamu Aboriginal people have a lovely Dreamtime legend: *A great sea turtle swallowed a large hot stone in her stomach. She then threw herself into the ocean and heated up the sea.* The village has three hot springs, which were discovered by Europeans in 1870 while searching for pasture land near Herbert River. The benefits of these thermal waters convince us to take two days' rest on the spot.

Once I have retrieved the rations that I have had sent ahead here, I swim in the hot springs, hoping to relieve my painful joints. A heavenly balm.

Mitch doesn't hesitate in taking the opportunity to join us for forty-eight hours, after a fourteen-hour drive. He brings supplies for the horses, and for us, too. I carry the least I can. We meet a hiker going down the Trail towards the south, crushed under the weight of his 20-kilogram backpack. We exchange information, and he asks me a million questions on what he's to expect from the road ahead.

On the 14th of June, we leave Innot Hot Springs. The weather is muggy. On the Tablelands, which reach 1046 metres at their highest point, nights are cold. But we get to enjoy a magnificent view on Mount Misery.

My fingers, my hands and my ankles hurt horribly, and I'm completely depleted. Shooting pain wrenches tears from my eyes. I can't walk normally anymore, and I rely much more on my three companions. When I get out of the saddle, I'm so stiff and sore that I have to wait a moment before being able to put a foot to the ground. But I learn to live with it. My pain threshold is getting higher, helping me to bite the bullet.

When I was a teenager, I fractured my lumbar vertebrae falling off my horse onto a tree stump in the forest. The military school people who were accompanying us ordered me back in the saddle. We returned to the stables after a long ride. I didn't complain and at the time I stupidly refused to have some X-rays done. Then, in India, when I was eighteen, I contracted dengue fever. I didn't tell my hosts about it straightaway and ended up spending three weeks in bed with a raging fever. I didn't want to be sent back to France – I was determined to travel through Rajasthan on horseback. But my family didn't let me do it, fearing for my health. I then experienced extreme cold in Mongolia, -20 degrees Celsius, when camping, feeding myself with dried meat. One day, having lost a lot of weight and all my strength, my body said 'stop' and refused to obey my commands. I crumpled into the snow, announcing that I couldn't get back on my horse. My partner, Damian, said simply, 'If you don't carry on, you'll die right here.' The reality of it was that simple.

We're reaching higher altitudes as we skirt the fertile plateau west of the Atherton Tablelands, part of the Great Dividing Range. This plateau retains small tropical forests of arborescent ferns, taller than me, and giant eucalypts. One of the most important bird reserves in the country, it's listed as a World Heritage site. I glimpse cranes with ash-coloured feathers and red heads, perched up on their high legs. The views are breathtaking: your gaze is snatched into infinity.

We ride by a very odd place, a kind of ghost village hanging on for dear life in the foothills of the Tablelands, where flourishing tin mines used to be. All that's left of them now are derelict buildings and an old station, with a few decrepit houses inhabited by folks who enjoy being off the grid. Time seems to have stopped in this place, buried in its dark forest, hanging onto the steep flank of a mountain. It would be well suited as a stage-set for a colonial-Australia movie.

The gloomy setting doesn't stop the pub owner from being welcoming. Cat and I enjoy a hamburger and a beer. In the past, in this remote and mountainous landscape, packhorses carried 80 tons of tin a month towards a foundry, where the ore was transformed into ingots and then conveyed on a small coal steam engine, named 'Betty', up to Stannary Hills. On the return journey, the wagons were loaded with supplies for the village. There, horses were bred for the army in India. It's dizzying to think of the importance such a small locality had during the settlers' time. One of its inhabitants was even a government minister for Queensland.

On the 15th of June, I realise, without being quite certain of it, that we've travelled beyond 5000 kilometres. I may not be counting my kilometres by the metre, but it's a fair number, even if our *final* objective is Cooktown. Cat and I are bivouacking near a lake. In the morning, we're entranced by the sunrise, in which the clouds, reflected in the water, seem to swim. It's a delight to be mesmerised by the humming, buzzing insect race taking place across the liquid surface.

According to my calculations, we're fifteen days from reaching that town with the mythical name. I take out the Section 1 map, the last of my trek on the BNT, and which we have been following backwards. The sky is blue, just shy of purple – it could be part of a 'Flemish primitives' painting. A gap in the trees is circled with incredibly fine and chiselled tufts of grass. Small shrubs, and the *black-boys* – with their diminutive trunks and headdresses of bushy green hair that

I love so much – contrast with the white trunks of the giant ghost gums opening their umbrellas of foliage against the dark hills speckled with lights. Such is the timeless work of art in front of us.

We start our descent of the Great Dividing Range, and come to an old tobacco, rice and fruit plantation. In Mutchilba, I have an appointment with a farrier: my team needs new shoes. One of his clients stops by, opportunely, and invites us to camp on her property. To get there, I ride bareback and Cat climbs into the farrier's four-wheel drive, and he asks her straight out: 'Are youse two a pair of carpet munchers?' Cat, being an Englishwoman, doesn't understand his lingo, and his Australian drawl doesn't help. Partially grasping 'munching', she assures him that we have both had enough to eat on the Trail. Seeing two young women travelling together, this Queenslander can't imagine any other scenario; he discovers his mistake, however, when Mitch turns up for a day's rest.

Three days later, we venture into even more remote and isolated places in the bush. Towards Mount Molloy, we're progressing along a peak on rocky paths in a landscape sculpted with gullies. Vegetation blocks our way – it's more and more difficult to get through. I lose time at a fork in the track, trying to understand the guide's some thirty-years-old reading. Frustrated, I decide to follow my nose, instead. Cat trusts me, but I soon start wondering if I'm not off-track …

In fact, we're quite lost. We progress haphazardly up steep paths, forever climbing and then diving down, in the direction that's supposed to lead us to a camp location. Cat, very red again, never complains. It's also hard on my horses. As for myself, I can hardly walk. After three hours of this blind, painful rambling, I must admit that we're going in the wrong direction. We've got to retrace our steps, but it's too late in the day to do so.

As I scan our surroundings, all I can see are small gullies where disgusting waters fester. I climb a small rise in search of another path. Cat has reached the limit of her strength. In spite of her resistance, I make her climb onto Roxanne and I continue on foot. We're both obstinate, and continue like this a few more kilometres. From another rise, I see some smoke far in the distance, which must be the old goldmine we are headed for. Before going back, it's imperative that I find some water. Coming to a ravine, I leave Cat and the horses there and set off on foot. Aboriginal people taught me that in the presence of large rocks, in general, you'll find water – and it works! I discover a large hole with clear water in it. I'm so relieved I could dance, but I husband my energy so I can get back to Cat. We set up our camp in the failing light. Our bad luck has, at least, brought us this unexpected haven.

At dawn, we start off without delay. We have to travel all the way back, in the opposite direction to yesterday. At the fork where I went astray, we follow the right path – hardly visible, drowned in scrub. We're heading towards Kingsborough, a benighted place, which on this day boasts a single inhabitant, a certain Ike Sjofors, who has taken on the banner of being the only one left. This old gold-digger, who came here thirty years ago, has created an oasis for himself, along with a vegetable garden, in the hope of attracting people to his small lost paradise in the middle of the bush – this human desert. Like in *The Desert of the Tartars*, he waits for someone to come to him. But he's still always there, alone.

We can hardly make out the path, taken over by the bush and which no-one uses anymore. Lured by the idea of stumbling on a unique, whimsical, even wonderful, location, we end up in quite an ordinary place. We must pay our due in order to step into Ike's domain – it's the only way to gain access to the water reserve he has made for himself; this bush hermit has his head firmly screwed onto his shoulders. Only, not many people come by this way. His spring will not bring the old gold-digger much ore.

We're climbing up towards Mount Molloy, a historic mining town with a population that has dwindled to 273 inhabitants. The mines are depleted, and the younger generation are moving to the cities. We're facing the temporary closure of the Trail, because there's no way through the bush. The BNT itinerary is a living thing. The conditions of access and the state of each place changes according to the guide book's updates and the weather conditions. It so happens that segments 10, 11, and 12, on the map to Mount Molloy, in the last passage in the guide, are closed. No track in sight. We've got no choice: we have to bush-bash our way towards the east if we want to reach the sea – which is waiting for us straight ahead.

Riding on to East Hodgkinson River, the land is dry, and when we find water it's a measly puddle. For a few days, my brumbies have had nothing to graze on. Unburdened of their loads, cleaned, petted and thanked, my three friends plonk themselves in front of us to beg for food, while Cat and I lunch on sardines and biscuits. I explain to them that I don't have anything left, but that they'll get something at Mount Molloy. I'm so ashamed to eat in front of them. It tears me apart not being able to meet their needs.

On a cloudy morning, under a solid drizzle, we leave the muddy puddle next to which we have spent the night. We follow the tracks of wild horses. The maps distances are approximate. Thankfully, after 5000 kilometres, I've become pretty handy at relating the mud maps to the country around me. My guidebook recommends travelling with a compass. From 1882 to 1891, horses from the company Cobb & Co. were the only means of transport in this area, using some six thousand horses to cover the country, which still remains inaccessible by car.

We ride across gullies till we reach the foothills of the mountains, submerged in tall grass. I can't see Cat. Not very tall, she wrestles with unfriendly bushes and with the rain, crying out from time to time when she loses sight of our tracks. I stop regularly to study the landscape and to try to compare it to my surveys, as the horses progress in single file over the difficult, scrubby terrain. I love this challenge of reading the landscape to navigate in the bush. There's no road, no path, nothing, *nada*.

After six hours of relentless bush-bashing, we arrive exactly at the place I had planned to find, on an old stone track, built by the settlers. We sway on our feet. Suddenly, the ears of my three companions perk up. I know there isn't a living soul where we are, but then a herd of wild bay brumbies scrambles from behind the bushes at a full gallop. My friends have recognised their brethren. We're coming out of Hann Tableland National Park, at the northern tip of Queensland. It offers us sumptuous visions of outcrops and rocky spurs as a parting gift.

Epic week! We're back on the Trail, in spite of the tall grasses, 'spear grasses', which are taller than my horses. In this so-little-travelled part of the Trail, vegetation is king. Walking on these chaotic paths with my weakened and inflamed joints, I've sprained my ankle good and proper. We camp on the shores of Mitchell River, among mobs of cattle, who keep the feed sparse. Squadrons of insects sting us and drive us round the bend. I spray a special insect repellent that contains essential oils on my companions, which should stop them from scratching themselves all night. Cat and I sleep covered from head to toe, wrapped up like mummies.

The next day, we reach Mount Molloy at last. The contrast is stunning. We ride on the side of the freeway, where bikers and trucks overtake us. After three weeks entirely alone in the bush, this township, tucked away in its own mining past, 50 kilometres from Cairns, embodies a return to civilisation. Mount Molloy is a tarred road, with a few houses and some electric poles dotted each side of it. In the past, a strong Chinese community grew vegetable gardens here to nourish the men who worked in the copper mines. A Trail coordinator welcomes us, and I go to the pub to retrieve the supplies I have had sent ahead. We leave two days later. The guidebook tells me there're eight days of trek left before we reach Cooktown, the final point of our odyssey.

Atop the Great Dividing Range, we travel east; which is to say, along the coast. The landscape has changed again. From dry, hard and rocky, it has morphed into green and lush tropical forests. Sugar cane, palm trees and creepers have replaced the austere and unforgiving bush. The Pacific Ocean is only a 'Bump Track' away, thought to have been an old Aboriginal hunting trail, and runs for 6 kilometres between sea and mountain. In the early days of colonisation, after the discovery of gold in the region in 1877, this track was a vital link between Port Douglas and the back country, both for the miners and the settlers. On this Bump Track, all the artillery and the explosives necessary for the back-country tin, copper and gold mines were transported by horses and oxen. A wagon of 4 tons had to be drawn by thirty-six horses. Many of them perished on the way. The path dives into a dense tropical forest of gigantic trees. I feel tiny in this dark jungle strewn with rays of light. The trees form a vault above us. The ferns, the creepers, the flying roots intertwine as we tackle our descent towards the coast. An opening in the trees gives us a glimpse of the ocean in the distance: a first on the Trail since our departure. This unprecedented view is a joy and a reassurance.

My three horses travel easily on this camel-back-shaped road. When we reach the foot of the mountains, civilisation appears as houses and roads, as well as crops, mostly of sugar cane. From Port Douglas to Mossman, we're constrained by having to follow Captain Cook Highway. The fast lanes, paralleled by a train track used for transporting sugar cane towards the refineries, are very dangerous for traffic.

On the 29th of June – seventy-six days since my return to the Trail and 389 days since our departure – we stop to take a breather, as with any other mode of transport, at a service station. I give my horses a drink under the watch of disbelieving drivers. I urge Cat to hitchhike, which will be less tiring. We have a big day to get through. As for me, 15 kilometres along the freeway with my three steeds requires all my concentration, and sometimes our trio slows down the traffic.

Once in Mossman, with its corrugated-iron roofs, its palm-tree lined streets and its two thousand inhabitants, we decide it's inviting enough for a break. We settle the brumbies in a rodeo ground, and Cat and I make do with the stables.

For several days now, my left heel has been hurting like the devil. I've got an angry rash, which is hot, enflamed and jabs me with sharp pains. I tell myself it will go on its own. In the desert, I had already contracted staphylococcus, and, in these last weeks, after stressing my body more than usual, my immune system has been cracking under the pressure. It could be a new staphylococcus, in which case it's doubtful it will go away on its own – as I so blithely suppose.

Pouring rain constrains us with having to stay four days in Mossman, where my brumbies take advantage of this pause to put some fat on their bones. Cat, who has other engagements, is miserable not to be able to stay with me, so close to the goal. Before her departure, we'd thought we'd camp on the beach, further north. When the rain abates a little one morning, we use the opportunity to take the horses to the sea.

That day, my foot is so painful that I go to the town's hospital. A boil has now appeared, and the doctor gives me antibiotics. A second boil, even larger than the last one, doubles the size of my leg. The wound isn't pretty; however, I'm far from giving up or slowing down. I ask the locals where we can set up on the beach – my absolute dream, camping on the beach with my horses, could be coming true.

The rain has stopped. We leave Mossman in the direction of Wonga Beach, on the Pacific Ocean, with its long stretch of sand. I've spotted a place under the palm trees lined with pasture and a freshwater stream, which can be reached by following the shore. After more than a year in the bush, this is just about wonderland. A white sandy beach dotted with palm trees and black rocks, facing the mountain in the distance – this suits me thoroughly, despite the crocodiles.

My foot hurts like hell, but I reassure myself that the antibiotics will do the trick. Camping by the water, however, I start wondering if the treatment is sufficient. I swim with my horses. Cat takes photographs of our last day together – this 4th of July – as she has to leave tomorrow. That night, the pain wakes me up, and Cat is distraught at the idea of leaving me like this. We're so sad to say goodbye. I'll never forget this woman.

A New Zealand man named Carl, living on the edge of the beach, offers to keep my equipment in his garage. He's a biker, strong, burly, and covered in tattoos from head to toe. He shelters me in his place for a night as if I were a member of his family. I can't sleep, and I cry with pain. I feel as if I were dying. I want to go to a hospital in Cairns, 94 kilometres from here. I must organise things: I put out a cry for help on social media and, in less than an hour, hundreds of people offer their assistance. A mother and her daughter take my horses to a paddock where they'll be safe. From afar, Mitch asks his boss, who's passing through here, to pick me up in his car and take me to the hospital in Cairns. The result of all this is that I spend three days in emergency care with an intravenous transfusion, before I'm given a room where I'm ordered to stay put, in order to avoid the infection reaching my tendons and my bones. In theory, I'm six days from the end of the Trail. At this late stage, it's frustrating to be lying here – miserable, on a hospital bed, with my ravaged face, black circles under my eyes, suffering acute pain, broken down, at a full stop. Furious with myself, powerless. My heart is broken over the fact that Cat and I couldn't finish the adventure together, but also overwhelmingly touched by the speed and number of all the responses to my SOS.

In a new development, the doctors lance the two boils, taking 2 centimetres of flesh off my left ankle and right leg. When I explain that I'm in a hurry, that I'm determined to finish the Trail, they ground me again, ordering me to stay in hospital until my two open wounds have healed. By the magic of chance encounters, a woman who has been following my blog is in the same hospital, on the floor below me. She has a broken leg from falling off her horse. We keep each other company.

As for Mitch, I find him by my bedside at dawn, having driven all night. He turns up the very day I've decided to leave the hospital. The care he surrounds me with stuns me. Against the doctors' advice, I leave the hospital with open wounds. Out at last, I tell myself it's a good thing to get some fresh air. To lift my spirits, before getting back on the Trail, Mitch organises to take me for a flight in one of the company's helicopters over the Great Barrier Reef. The largest coral reef in the world, it's visible below the turquoise water, which turns violet-blue as you reach the high seas. An offer to see one of nature's marvels can't be turned down, even with a bandaged foot and leg.

Then the time comes to return to my three companions. I hobble along. Mitch has brought me some Crocs, which I can slip on easily – actually, I can't wear anything else. I'm a week late for the film crew's schedule; they had organised to record my arrival in Cooktown. I learn that the name of the town is in memory of James Cook, who explored the Pacific and whose three-masted ship, *Endeavour*, ran aground on the reef.

Mitch travels with me to Daintree, at the heart of Australia's tropical forest, probably the oldest in the world – a sanctuary where one can feel what the earth was like during the time of the dinosaurs. World Heritage listed, it contains

90 per cent of the existing species of bats and butterflies in the country, and more than twelve thousand species of insects, as well as cassowaries. The high levels of humidity in the air are prohibitive for the healing of my wounds, and my leg is wrapped in a plastic bag. It takes us three days to reach Daintree River, the river where I'm to meet the film crew. Erica is here, too, to guide them through this part of the world.

My troubles aren't over. This last section is replete with challenges. One of them is the crossing of the Daintree River, teeming with saltwater crocodiles – the largest, the most aggressive and dangerous of their kind. They're about 6 metres long and weigh up to a tonne. The river is 140 kilometres wide in some sections. Its source is at 110 metres altitude in the Daintree National Park's 140,000-year-old, 120,000-hectare tropical forest. It then flows into the Pacific Ocean.

We start off with the CREB Track, a challenge of 71 kilometres, which has the reputation of being the steepest, most rugged and adventure-packed track, and the hardest to access, for four-wheel drives in the whole of Australia. It runs from Daintree to Wujal Wujal, the only possible route to Cooktown for the electrical power services.

The track looks like a roller-coaster. Slippery because of the weather conditions, it's temporarily closed to four-wheel drives, which stops the film crew from following me; my horses and I get special permission from the council to travel on it. Two days are spent in Daintree fine-tuning the complex logistics, so that the film crew can shoot the crossing of the river and meet up with us for the last three days of the Trail. Even right to the end, this whole adventure is a battle. I desperately need to finish this ultimate challenge. All I want is to get going and to not have to worry about the film crew anymore. I'm just sad that I have to leave Mitch, and he's not even sure he will be able to be there for our arrival in Cooktown, at the extreme north of the country between the mouth of the Daintree River and Cape Tribulation.

We set off to cross the Daintree. The film crew is waiting for us on the shore, and is talking with a group of tourists who are looking for the safest passage according to the river flow. The ford we should have used to cross is about 20 metres long and the flow is turbulent. I can't see the river bottom and, for added spice, the locals inform me that a crocodile has made himself at home at this precise point of passage. Nobody is feeling very safe about it. My intention to cross the Daintree with my three brumbies worries the whole crew. They all insist that I shouldn't do this just to satisfy the camera operators.

I'm not ready to throw in the towel, but I don't want to run any risks with my horses' lives. A small barge, belonging to a couple who live in the area, goes by and moors by the shore. As I wish to discover the depth of the river, with the intention of assessing the best point of passage, the owner invites me on board. From there, I can approximately guess where the flow isn't so powerful. I know that riders have lost their mounts on the Trail by crossing tempestuous rivers with a powerful flow. I ask the barge owner if he wouldn't mind transporting my pack saddle, which is heavy and cumbersome – a real handicap in conditions such as these – as well as Fox, and he accepts. My leg is still wrapped in a garbage bag and duct tape; I don't look all that flash hobbling about. After taking a long while to reflect, I ride Roxanne into the churning waters, my feet lifted as high as possible. I press my horses on: there's no need to delay at this delicate juncture. The crew films our crossing. We get to the other shore in one piece, and my faithful friends haven't batted an eyelid. Happy about the outcome of this episode, which wasn't a sure thing, I retrieve my equipment from the barge, and saddle my packhorse, not regretting setting off on our own again, now that the film crew has been left on the other shore.

I worry about another last challenge: climbing this closed roller-coaster track, which is steep, and slippery after three days' rain on clay soil. I've lost a lot of time discussing and negotiating. The hours have been ticking by and I don't want to linger anymore. We start the ascent, and gain altitude very quickly. The red-and-yellow dirt path climbs and, when you look up, it seems to fly through the dense forest. My brumbies' resilient agility impresses me once again. They don't stumble on this slippery ground. They never panic, and I'm always in the saddle because I can't walk. As we progress over a particularly steep spot, I suddenly hear the roar of motocross bikes. The bikers are doing the climb on the opposite side, in spite of the track being closed. My heart is thumping at the idea of a collision. I make an about-turn, trying to find an opening in the jungle where I might take refuge with my friends. Luckily, we just make it off the narrow track when the bikes come roaring up the hill. I speak to my horses to keep them calm. When they appear, we're only two metres away from each other. But they stop immediately when they see us. It has been a close shave. These mechanical horses could have spelt panic to my flesh-and-blood ones or they could have run us over.

The descent is much rougher. My horses land, and slide, on their backsides. All I can do is rely on them and on their good-will. I'm still in the saddle; my brumbies are carrying me on this part of the trek. I'm so proud of them and of their dexterity in handling this difficult terrain. I love this very, very beautiful final part of the Trail. The air is hot and moist. I'm happy, though, because we're going to find a good place to camp for my three friends.

We're climbing again. My horses are dripping with sweat, but never balk at anything. They have a marvellous talent for adaptation and are really able to handle any terrain. The view from the summit is magnificent. On the ground, I see crossroads of wild boar tracks – there must be swarms of them. I've managed to keep my foot and leg dry, and every day I rigorously bandage my wounds. I've been out of hospital for four days now.

I've chosen a location that's not too humid and has some grass for us to settle our camp in. Days of rain have drenched the earth. I manage to find some dry wood by breaking dead branches from trees, and build up a hell of a fire so I can dry out the sweat-saturated saddle-pads, my clothes, and, very importantly, my socks.

The river isn't that close, and I limp there to get some water. I can hear hundreds of birds singing their heads off.

Apart from heavy circles under my eyes, I seem to be okay – to be holding on. The horses rest with me. I explain to them that we only have four days left before reaching our goal. Though I'm keen to get to the end of our adventure, I savour this night camping in the heart of a tropical forest, with my brumbies and Fox at my side. The swish of winged insects, the frogs, the rustle of the enormous night-butterfly wings, the strident parrot cries, the cracking of branches, the flutter of bats in flight: the thick soundtrack of the living jungle. Nature's mesmerising melodies in concert. And the forest kingdom is not only about sound. The density, the lushness of its preserved plant life is stamped on my senses forever.

Feeling like a female Crusoe, I wonder if I enjoy it here so much because I know I'm reaching the end of our adventure or because I've never experienced such an extraordinarily beautiful forest, abounding with animal and vegetal life. Perhaps this feeling also comes to me because I dared to leave the hospital. Whatever it is, I enjoy the gift of this enchanted moment. This track lined with tropical plants is my reward for all I've gone through.

As we descend an abysmally steep slope, the views are dizzying. I'm so happy to have taken on this closed section, in spite of my leg and my painful foot, in spite of the Ross River fever and my aching joints, in spite of my exhaustion and the slippery ground. Apart from the brief encounter with the motocross bikers, we're alone in the world of this gigantic virgin forest.

My horses, sweating and agile, carry on, adaptable as ever. Now and then, we travel under a ceiling of foliage that seals off the light. We cross small cascades, several fords. The sound of lapping water is so heavenly.

I meet Erica and the film crew, who have wisely made the detour at the foot of the track. We're now three days from Cooktown – three days that will reveal themselves to be frustrating. The camera crew constantly ask me to repeat the difficult passages, to cross fords again, and in the state I'm in this amounts to a superhuman effort. I had also asked them to bring feed for my horses – and they forgot. We finish the CREB Track by arriving at Bloomfield River. Here, the valleys abound with streams. At last, I get onto the large road leading to Cooktown. These efforts, combined with the antibiotics, have shattered me. My legs can hardly carry me anymore, and I find myself in a camp chosen by the camera crew, which irritates me and only adds to my exhaustion.

The eve before crossing the finishing line, we're in a pub, The Lion's Den Hotel, positioned on the side of the road – a pleasant hundred-year-old establishment. I don't start celebrating because, in the middle of the day, I noticed that Cooper has managed to lose a shoe. I ask myself what more could happen before we reach the endpoint of our journey. Cooper can't walk 30 kilometres on a tarmacked road without a shoe! At the pub, always the hub of local life, I find a farmer who offers to change it for him.

Stepping out of the pub, I meet a woman called Sue, in her thirties, carrying a little girl on her hip, who's passionate about horses. She understands I'm at the end of my rope and proposes a paddock on her property for my companions. We get there and I sleep on the spot, free from the film crew. Sue, her five daughters, running barefoot, and her husband live in a shed with their horses – so, I have discovered another unique family who have adapted their way of life to their passion. Till the end, the Trail has fostered such interesting encounters.

An ultimate mishap: I had organised for a truck to bring my three horses from Cooktown to the south, but at the last minute, the driver lets me down because of a lack of clients that far north. Over the phone, Mitch proposes to return to Emerald, a town with 11,000 inhabitants, in the heart of Queensland, in the Tropic of Capricorn, some 1000 kilometres from here – nothing less. He wants to borrow a truck and meet us at our arrival in Cooktown, at the point in which our odyssey will have ended once and for all. The trip entails spending thirty hours behind the wheel on a two-day journey. His offer leaves me speechless – it's so unreasonable and formidable …

This three-year chapter of my life will soon be coming to a close. I haven't thought about what I'll do after I'm done with the Trail. There's no doubt, the fear of returning to 'normal' life has me worried about facing a big void.

When I was at the hospital, the director of an endurance horse race in Mongolia, the Gobi Desert Cup, contacted me with the intention of sponsoring me. She wants me to take part in it to promote the race's inauguration. In exchange, she asks me to contribute to her competition, which is in its first run. Her proposal seduces me, in spite of my physical condition. It furnishes me with an excellent way to readjust, and should help me land smoothly on my feet. This horse endurance race extends over 580 kilometres across the Gobi, and is the second-longest and most difficult race of its kind. It starts off at the beginning of September, which would give me a month to get back on my feet and train. I see a double advantage: first, it tempts me; second, it offers me a transition. Two days before arriving in Cooktown, I accept the proposal to enter into this necessary adventure. The sequel to my initiatory voyage through the bush has been decided, and I won't suddenly find myself in a vacuum.

As I ride Roxanne towards the town with its legendary name, of which I have dreamed so often, I'm full of hope. My heart is surging with relief – nothing can stop us now. It's the 20th of July. I've just traversed 98 days of hell, for a total of 441 days, driven by the desire to reach our goal. No-one will ever quite know what I've been through, nor what I have endured. I can sense in my being the physical trace of every effort this expedition has demanded of me: 5330 kilometres travelled, thirteen months of peregrination, and a life suspended in time. It feels totally unreal to be in this moment – totally insane. We've reached the last leg of our big challenge. We've won! It's windy, my new hat, adorned with its newly found feathers, is screwed tight on my head. I'm attached to those feathers – they're my talismans. The horses hasten to a trot. They understand we're arriving. Roxanne picks up her step at the excitement in my voice. Fox gambols around, leading the way. On the tarmacked road, people are driving fast, but we don't care. Nothing can mar our joy. I yell out, howling, yet again like a dingo.

I've reached this extremity of the world, where the earth touches the sea. I'm so grateful to Australia for being the country that has given me the strength and the energy to bring this adventure to its fruition. I'm so grateful to Australia for showing me the true splendour of its land. I haven't vanquished the Trail; it has led me through it. I haven't conquered the immensity of the bush, but it lives within me now.

On the outskirts of the town, a group of riders are expecting me – women and children, most of them strangers, who followed our journey on social media. I'm moved to tears by this surprise welcome. We cross the town until we reach the plaque signalling the start of the Trail. In front of the pub – because everything always finishes in a pub – people are clapping. Erica and the film crew are expecting me near the arrival stele stone. She crowns me with a glitzy fake tiara, and we share a wink.

When I climb out of the saddle, it's hard not to sob. I cannot believe it. Limping, hobbling and swaying, my foot wrapped in plastic, I thank my heroes, my brumbies, who brought me back. I thank Erica and the Guy Fawkes Heritage Horse Association, as well as the people who have come to welcome me from far and wide. Among them is Mitch, the man who supported me with his strength, his devotion and his tenderness. I realise what it must have taken for him to be here. In this same moment I catch my family on the phone. All those who supported me are in my thoughts. My heart is full.

We've managed it! I never want to put a pack saddle on Roxanne's, Cooper's or River's backs again – my beloved brumbies. I wouldn't be without them for all the gold in China.

Before setting off for Ulan Bator, there is somewhere essential I have to go to. Mitch has come in the truck he managed to wrangle, to transport us all – me, my horses and my beloved Fox – and take us back, not to Dorrigo this time, but to his home. We've decided to live together. The Trail has united us. I met Mitch because my route went past his door. He was there fortuitously. Now, we're returning to where our story started. It's not *down the road,* either. As usual in Australia, the distances are enormous. Mitch's parents' property is 1600 kilometres from the north end of the BNT. It takes us several days to reach south-east Queensland, five hours north of Brisbane. Their home is a cattle station, with some two thousand heads of cattle, raised on a bit over 4000 hectares of hilly country extending as far as the eye can see. To the European that I am, this life is in a remote world. The isolation is total, the first village an hour away by car. To reach their previous property, far out west, his father had used a plane he keeps in a small hangar, but which they now enjoy for smaller trips and leisure. I'm welcomed with warmth and simplicity. No-one asks me questions. Max, Mitch's father, comes from a Scottish settler family. Mona, his mother, is of Norwegian descent. They are both tireless workers, which doesn't stop them from gazing upon the world and loving travel. This seventy-year-old man, with piercing blue eyes and a white beard, is as thin as an athlete. He's a man of few words, and with a wealth of deadpan humour. Mona is in her sixties, tiny, cheerful and natural, never without a smile on her face. Both adopt me and make me feel at home. The house stands on top of a hill; it's covered in bougainvillea, surrounded by a pristine lawn and a white picket fence, to keep the many dogs, hens, and guineafowl, who chase the snakes, at a distance. The station is called Hazeldean, and seems a paradise. Mitch takes me to visit every corner of it. I discover a little more each day. A real bushman, he's as comfortable on a horse as in a helicopter. He can do anything with his hands, and when he's not competent about something he learns it on the spot. He loves everything mechanical and the refurbishing of all kinds of vehicles fascinates him, expending reserves of energy on minutiae and precision. After several years wandering in the bush, in Aboriginal communities, and through many adventures, I feel I've reached a haven. I'm ready to drop my backpack and live with this man who supported my freedom without any demands. I had reached the end of the rope before Mitch came to get me. He gave me back life – our life.

But I must drag myself away. I have committed myself to running in this endurance race in Mongolia, and I mustn't let the grass grow under my feet if I want to be ready for it. The symptoms from the Ross River fever have not left my body, and my joints are still painful. I leave my horses at the farm. I don't need them, and it's a good thing – they deserve their rest. The mounts are provided by the race's organisation. Then, against all expectations, but probably because I've been seasoned by my year's ride through the bush, I win the endurance race in Mongolia.

The Mongolian steppes make me yearn for my family, whom I haven't seen for a long time. With no more engagements, I return to France, but within two months I am missing Mitch terribly. He comes over to join me. It's an opportunity for him to meet my parents and siblings. I take advantage of this to have him discover France, which he has never seen. He's genuinely fascinated by its history, going so far back in time. The Mont Saint-Michel stuns him. The fact that it was first built in the ninth century, when the oldest buildings in Australia are only two hundred years old, is an added wonder for him.

I love my family and France, but my life is elsewhere now, and I return to Australia to live with Mitch. As a helicopter pilot, he needs to move around a lot, and I give up my job in the Aboriginal communities to follow him on his trips. I go on several missions with him, before we decide to settle ourselves at the family farm. Since then, I help his parents with the farm, and work on neighbouring farms, too. I love looking after the animals. I would like to train my horses to muster cattle, and to get to ride Roxanne, River and Cooper for work and for pleasure. My companions roam free in the paddock in front of the house. I see them every morning when I open my curtains. Roxanne comes to check on me at the window when I'm in the kitchen, eyeing my movements in case I have a treat for her. I see them feasting on mangoes – the house is surrounded with mango trees. When I call them, they run up, and they recognise the sound of my car. They're always hanging around, to get some pats. I will never leave them. Along with Fox, they are my family.

One evening under the stars, when we're camping on Kolan River at the exact same place we met, Mitch asks me to marry him. The wedding is very quiet. We're barefoot under one of the farm's trees, surrounded by his family and mine, Roxanne, Cooper, River and Fox. And also ours – because I'm six months pregnant and we're expecting a boy.

Acknowledgements

I thank everyone who helped me on my adventure. Firstly, Erica and Graeme from the Guy Fawkes Heritage Horse Association from NSW. They supported me from day one to the very end – helped me acquire my horses, homed me and mentored me through their training, and supported me the entire duration of my adventure as my expedition managers.

I'd also like to thank Kate Young, and Arnold and Sally Duckett from the same association.

Thank you to the Aboriginal community Docker River in the Northern Territory where I discovered the bush and my first brumbies.

Thank you also to the following people.

My mother. My family, les Gouvello and the tontine.

Gilles and Jean who believed in my dream.

Everyone who donated to my GoFundMe site.

Everyone I met on the road, who supported me, fed me, gave me a shower, a bed or made me smile in a difficult time. Special thanks to Finnie, Emilie, Kathryn and Preston, Belinda and many more, my trail angels.

Everyone who supported me on social media with their messages of encouragement.

Calibre Aviation for their truck and getting me to hospital.

The families who looked after my horses when I went to hospital.

The farriers and vets who came to find me in rural places, especially Nathan Jessup.

The Lynas family of East Coast Horse Transport.

The photographers Ellen Keidge and in particular Cat Vinton who followed me on foot for six weeks when I was in paralysing pain due to Ross River tropical fever. Her presence and support were a god's send.

Damian Smerdon and Debra Novak for their videos.

Kaufman Productions for believing in me.

Australian Geographic and *Sidetracked Magazine* for their funding.

My sponsor Alpkit for their camping gear.

My saddlers John Burton and the Overseer at Armidale.

Denis Demonpion.

Christian Bex.

My Australian publishers, Affirm Press.

Catherine de Saint Phalle.

Jean-Louis Gouraud for introducing me to my French publisher, Arthaud.

The National Trail Coordinators, Hazel and Martin at Oberon, Louise and Bill at Kangaroo Hill and Craig and Shirley at Marlborough.

And a final thank you to Mitch without whom I may not have reached the end of my expedition with my tropical fever.